Photoshop 7 Trade Secrets

Janee Aronoff
David Cross
Gavin Cromhout
Colin Smith

Photoshop 7 Trade Secrets

© 2002 friends of ED

First Printed September 2002

Trademark Acknowledgements

Published by friends of ED

30-32 Lincoln Road, Olton, Birmingham.
B27 6PA. UK.
Printed in USA

ISBN 1-903450-91-8

Credits

Authors
Janee Aronoff
Dave Cross
Gavin Cromhout
Colin Smith

Additional Contributors & Reviewers
Josh Fallon
Denis Graham

Commissioning Editor
Ben Renow-Clarke

Technical Editor
Libby Hayward

Managing Editor
Anthea Elston

Project Managers
Richard Harrison, Jennifer Harvey

Graphic Editors
Katy Freer
Avtar Bhogal

Indexer
Fiona Murray

Proof Readers
Anthea Elston
Ben Renow-Clarke

Special Thanks
Julie Closs
Alan McCann

Janee Aronoff

I'm Janee Aronoff, teacher, author, and Photoshop Goddess. I live and work on the internet, mainly from my Photoshop resource web site, myJanee.com. My experience includes teaching high school mathematics, working in sales and marketing management, and beginning and operating a small bakery business.

Besides the writing that I did for Trade Secrets, in retouching and special effects, I have authored three chapters of Photoshop 7: Professional Photographic Techniques, written and maintained my acclaimed and well-visited myJanee.com, and written and sent over 3000 different e-mails in the past year.

I believe that everything we see physically is expressible in pixels. I believe that, since no one else has your vision, no one else can do your art. And I believe that perfectionism is the perfect obstacle to a meaningful and productive life. Don't do your best. Just DO.

Always me, Janee

Gavin Cromhout

Gavin Cromhout lives in Cape Town, South Africa and by a string of coincidences, has done so all his life. He studied both art and psychology at the University of Cape Town, taking psychology to a postgraduate level. You can catch up with him at http://www.lodestone.co.za.

Dave Cross

Dave Cross is an author and trainer based in Ottawa, Canada. He is the author and co-author of several Photoshop books and is a contributing writer to Photoshop User Magazine. Over the past 12 years Dave has trained thousands of users in graphics, publishing and web design. He is a member of the Photoshop World Instructor Dream Team, teaches for the Photoshop Seminar Tour and was named as one of Wacom's Top 40 Photoshop Experts. Dave is an Adobe Certified Expert, Certified Techical Trainer, Adobe Certified Training Provider and is often referred to by his students as "The Photoshop Coach".

Colin Smith

Colin Smith is an award winning Graphic Designer who has caused a stir in the design community with his stunning photorealistic illustrations composed entirely in Photoshop. He is also founder of the popular PhotoshopCafe web resource for Photoshop users and web designers. His images have been featured on the National Association of Photoshop Professionals web site.

He has won numerous design contests and awards, including the Guru Award at the 2001 Photoshop World Convention in LA. Colin's work has been recognized by Photoshop User, Mac Design, Dynamic Graphics, and WWW Internet Life magazines. Colin is also listed in the International Who's Who of Professional Management, and is an active member of NAPP. He is also a regular columnist for Planet Photoshop, and has moderated their web site forum.

3: Layers   71

4: Retouching 97

5: Special Effects
131

6: Web Graphics   161

7: Setting up

197

8: Hardware options   227

Welcome

How do you get the best out of Photoshop? It's a combination of knowing what you want and knowing how to do it properly: a mixture of creativity and acumen. As you learn more, you make fewer mistakes, your workflow becomes faster, and you have more time to explore creative possibilities. This book is dedicated to showing you the tricks of the trade, to sharing the insider's knowledge which will speed up your work, and to improving your understanding of Photoshop as a tool.

The book is divided into eight chapters, in the first three we look at ways of improving your efficiency, good selection techniques, and how to use layers effectively. In the next three chapters we look at practical applications of Photoshop for retouching and correction, Web graphics and special effects. As the emphasis of these chapters is project based, you will notice that these chapters have more practical exercises than in the rest of the book. The final two chapters look at the practicalities of Photoshop's configuration and hardware. Throughout the book, we cover the new features of Photoshop 7, so if you're not yet up to speed with the latest version, we'll show you the way.

To get the most information out of each of the authors that we possibly could, we used a collaborative method of writing. Each of the four authors chose two subject areas to be the main writer on, and once they had finished writing the sections, they were passed on to the other three authors for them to add their own tips and tricks to. All these parts then went out to review, and the reviewers (themselves Photoshop users) added their tips to the tip–tank. All of these tips then came together in editorial, where they were ordered and polished. In this way, we hoped to maximize the amount of insightful and essential information, and to give you the greatest benefit.

Layout conventions

This book is designed to be user-friendly, each chapter is packed with tips and advice, and you can choose to either dip in and out of each chapter, or to work through the book in order. To keep things simple we have used a handful of layout styles, which we'll run through now:

Each individual tip will appear under the following type of heading:

Wicked tip

Some of these tips are presented as small exercises, and in the time-honored fashion we have numbered each step, like this:

1. First do this,

2. Then do this

3. Next, do this, etc...

You'll notice that as well as the main tips, each chapter is jam-packed with helpful hints, which have been highlighted in the following way:

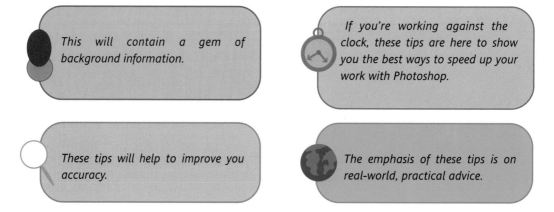

This will contain a gem of background information.

If you're working against the clock, these tips are here to show you the best ways to speed up your work with Photoshop.

These tips will help to improve you accuracy.

The emphasis of these tips is on real-world, practical advice.

As you'd expect in a book dedicated to efficiency, throughout the book we've included all the useful keyboard shortcuts that you'll need. These are presented with the Windows shortcut first and Mac second. Mac users beware; the OPTION key here is referred to as ALT – in line with most modern keyboards. Here is an example

To view an image at Actual Pixels size click CTRL/CMD+ALT+0.

When you come upon an important word or tool for the first time it will be in bold type:

Open the **Gradient Editor**

All menu commands are shown in the following way:

Go to **Image > Adjust > Hue/Saturation**

And finally, we've used different fonts to highlight filenames and URL's:

`Picture.psd` and www.friendsofed.com

Support

None of the exercises covered in this book are dependent on a specific source file, so feel free to use any of your own images. You will see that in many cases the authors have used images from the Adobe Photoshop 7 Stock art library, which ships with Photoshop 7. If you would like to use our original files, then you can download many of these images from www.friendsofed.com.

If you have any queries about this book, or friends of ED in general, then please visit our web site, you'll find a range of contact details there, or you can mail support@friendsofed.com, We'll be happy to deal with any technical problem quickly and efficiently.

There are lots of other features on the site that may interest you – interviews with top designers, samples from all our books, and a message board where you can post queries or join in with the discussions. If you have any comments please contact us – we'd love to hear from you!

1: Efficiency

We all love Photoshop – it's great, it's fun, it lets us create amazing graphics, but... But, well, it can be just a little bit frustrating can't it? Have you ever waited ages for an image to load because the file size was too big? Or opened completely the wrong image twenty zillion times because you can't remember how you named your images? Photoshop is such a huge application that using it can sometimes be a little laborious. Well, not any more folks. This chapter will look at the best ways of speeding up your Photoshop use from file organization to customizing the tools, we'll also look at faster previews, transforms and navigation, and we'll round off the chapter with a rundown of the best, most indispensable Photoshop shortcuts.

Many of the new additions to Photoshop 7 are dedicated to improving efficiency, so let's kick off the chapter by looking at these, starting with the File Browser and moving on to creating custom presets.

Enter the File Browser

One of the most celebrated features of Photoshop 7 is the File Browser. The File Browser is a multi-talented beast, it allows you to open, save, rename, and organize all your images with unprecedented ease. Let's explore the best ways to use this feature.

1. You can launch the browser from the palette well. If it's not visible, choose **Window > File Browser**, or simply choose **File > Browse**. The keyboard shortcut is SHIFT+CTRL/CMD+O.

1

2. You will then see the File Browser appear in the middle of the screen.

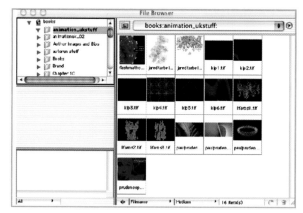

3. To take control over your desktop: Click on the top left arrow and choose **Dock to Palette Well** from the drop-down menu.

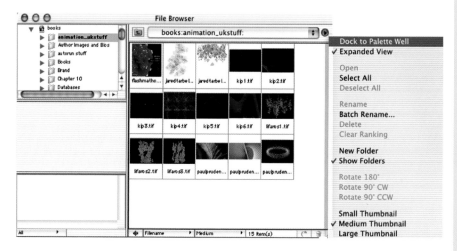

4. The File Browser will now be docked to the palette well. When you open an image the browser will be minimized in the well.

Opening multiple images

What if you want to open more than one image? Hold down the ALT key when you double-click a thumbnail. The image will open in Photoshop and the File Browser will remain open ready for further instructions. When you open your last image just double-click the thumbnail, the image will open and the File Browser will be nicely tucked away into the palette well.

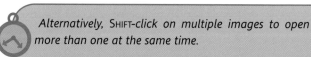

Alternatively, SHIFT-click on multiple images to open more than one at the same time.

Rotating images

Sometimes scanned images or images imported from a digital camera don't have the correct orientation. Previously you had to open them in Photoshop, rotate canvas and resave. This process could take a while depending on the size of the image.

Not anymore! Just click on the rotation arrow at the bottom of the File Browser palette.

Each time you click the image will be rotated 90 degrees clockwise. Press the ALT key to rotate counterclockwise.

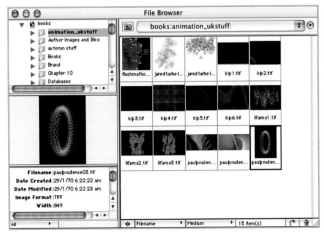

Not only will the image appear with the correct orientation in the thumbnail, it will open the right way up when you launch the document in Photoshop. This not only saves time, but also saves your image quality by avoiding a resample.

Renaming images

Another strength of the File Browser is the ability to rename images quickly.

Click on the name on the thumbnail and the name will be highlighted. Type in the new name and it will be renamed on the hard drive.

Press the TAB key to move to the next file name, or press SHIFT+TAB to move backwards between file names.

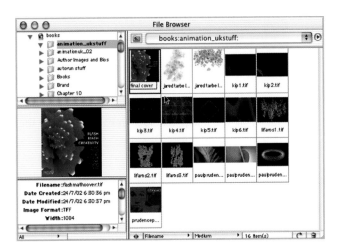

1

Renaming entire picture collections

When importing images from a digital camera you may have noticed the filenames don't mean much to you. If you have a few collections it will be difficult to locate an image by its cryptic name. Luckily there is a useful feature that will help you organize your images, called **Batch Rename**.

1. Select the images you want to affect by CTRL/CMD clicking, or choose the entire directory by choosing **Select All**, from the drop-down menu.

   The selected images will have a thick border to indicate they are selected.

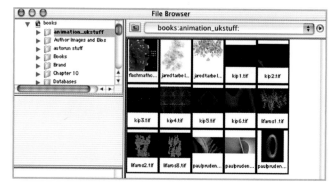

2. In the drop-down choose **Batch Rename**.

   You will now have several options. You can overwrite the filenames in the same folder, or if you want to make copies, choose **Move to new folder** and choose an alternative location. There are many options for the extensions that include date, filename, extension, 1 digit serial number, 2 digit serial numbers, and so on.

3. Choose a naming convention which suits you. Here I entered **barcelona + extension + 1 Digit Serial Number.** This will rename my pictures to: barcelona.tif.1, barcelona.tif.2... etc. Which makes a lot more sense. You can see a sample filename shown here.

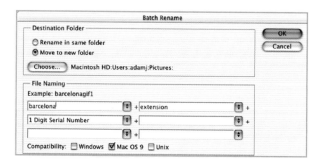

You could use all six naming options at once, to give you barcelona1a01b.tif, just in case you have a complicated series of photos that need detailed categorization.

If you have a whole series of images from a digital camera, you may want to rank them to help you decide which images you want to use. To do this in the File Browser, RIGHT/CTRL-click on an image and choose a Rank from A to E. Once you've ranked all the images, use the popup menu at the bottom to change the sorting from Filename (the default sorting method) to Rank. The images will display in order of ranking, regardless of their file names.

1

Optimizing Photoshop

One of the strengths of Photoshop is that it can be optimized to suit your needs, both through judicious use of the preloaded settings, and by customizing the tools and settings. This is covered in more detail in the **Setting Up** chapter; here we'll look at practical ways in which these custom tools can improve our efficiency.

Photoshop style sheets

Photoshop doesn't ship with any text style sheet options, right? Wrong. By using the new tool sets we can create our own text style sheets.

1. Start by applying the desired text to your image.

2. Apply the text and, with the Type tool still selected, click on the box in the top left of the Options bar. The Tool Preset box will drop-down. Select **Current Tool Only** to show only the text options and hide all the other Tool Presets.

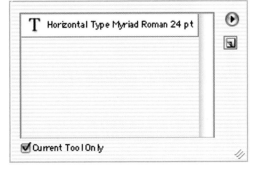

3. Click the arrow on the top right and choose **New Tool Preset** for the drop-down.

1

4. Give it a title, this one is called "White Text". You will see your new preset appear in the list.

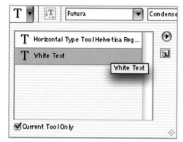

When you enter some text and change the options, Photoshop will use the most recent settings.

Here we want to make changes to the font, size and color. So we need to select the Type tool and choose our White Text preset.

Begin to type and notice all our settings are recalled.

This is particularly useful if you have a regular ad or web client that has a specific style of text. Simply name it after the client, etc. to have quick access.

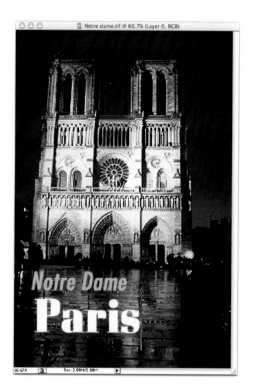

Using Tool Presets to help work group management

It's commonplace for several people to share the same workstation and each want to add notes to a group project. Create Tool Presets for the **Notes** tool with their names as the author, and they'll avoid having to change the settings back and forth on the Options bar.

1

Defining custom brushes

You can create a custom brush out of any picture.

1. Open your picture or create one. Here, you can see that my image is on a transparent background, for your image, you may need to select the area that you want to use as your brush. If you are using the whole image then press CTRL/CMD+A to select all.

2. To define the brush choose **Edit > Define Brush**.

3. When the dialog box pops up, name it and you are done.

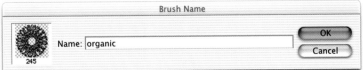

4. To use the brush, click B *for* the Brush tool, and choose the new brush from the menu.

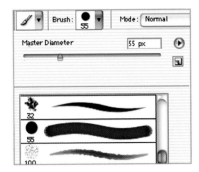

5. You will see the outline of your shape. Click once to apply the brush. Paint patterns with your new brush. The brushes support 256 levels of gray and one color.

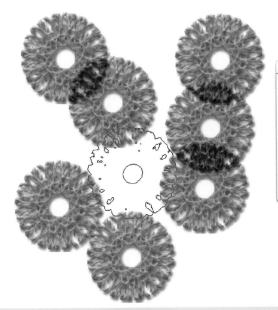

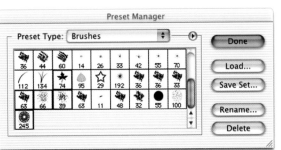

1

Brush shortcuts

- To change brush size on the fly, press the bracket keys: [to make the brush smaller,] to make the bush larger.

- In the Brushes palette, you can either view all the check boxes, options and sliders, or choose to just show the brushes themselves. To toggle between these two views select **Expanded View** from the Brushes palette popup menu.

- To quickly choose different brushes while you're using a tool, right/CTRL-click on your image and hold the mouse button. When the Brushes palette appears, click and drag onto the brush and then let go. In one step you'll have opened the Brushes palette, chosen a different brush and closed the palette again.

- To create a custom set of brushes that is a subset of the existing brushes, go to the **Edit > Preset Manager**. Choose Brushes from the Preset Type, then SHIFT-click to select all the brushes you want in your custom set. Finally click the Save Set button and name your set. You can also change the order of the brushes (or any other preset for that matter) in the Preset Manager. Simply click and drag a brush, swatch, pattern, etc to change the order. (To move multiple items, SHIFT-click on them and then drag as a group to change their order).

- To quickly change the opacity of any painting tool, first you need to have the tool selected, and then simply press 1 for 10% opacity, 2 for 20% and so on up to 90%. Press 0 to return to 100%. If you have the Move tool selected, the same keys will change the layer opacity rather than the tool opacity.

Previewing images

Many Photoshop users regularly perform what I call the palette shuffle, where you spend a good deal of your time moving, closing, reopening, collapsing, and enlarging palettes, in an effort to maximize the available screen space. Although that method certainly works, it may not be the most efficient technique. You can use Preview modes to make life with palettes a little easier.

There are different Preview modes available in Photoshop. You can access these simply by pressing the F key. Here is the standard view.

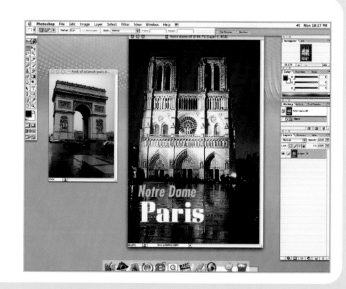

Press F to hide the Windows or Macintosh status bars.

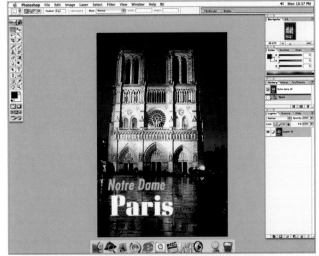

Press the F key again to hide the Photoshop menu bars.

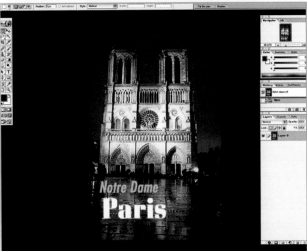

Now press CTRL/CMD+R to hide the rulers and the tab key to hide all the tool bars. We now have a full screen preview. Look, Mom - no clutter!

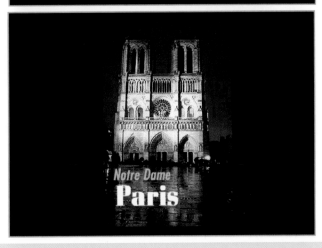

1

Press the F key again to bring back the standard preview and the TAB to show the toolbars and palettes again.

- To change the screen view of all open documents, hold down SHIFT when you click on the Screen mode button (the F shortcut won't work).

- To keep the toolbox and hide all other floating palettes, press SHIFT+TAB. To show them again, repeat the same shortcut. This can be very useful when you're working with a large image and you want to Fit on Screen (CTRL/CMD+ O) and/or zoom in. By hiding the floating palettes, you'll have more room for your image. To use a palette, just press SHIFT+TAB, use the palette, then press SHIFT+TAB again.

- To switch between open documents, press CTRL/CMD+TAB.

- Combine these two shortcuts to quickly create a slide show to look at your images without palettes or menus: F, F, CTRL/CMD+TAB; press F, TAB to get back to standard view.

Using dual monitors

Dual monitors provide a brilliant, but very expensive, solution to the floating palette syndrome. All that is needed is a graphics card that supports dual monitors and the drivers will allow setup. Oh, and of course another monitor! This is a fantastic boon, since you can literally move ALL of your floating palettes over to the other screen, leaving only the toolbar and your image. This really helps productivity. You can also keep your main monitor at your preferred display settings (say, 1024X768) and the other at a different setting (maybe standard default 800X600) and can see how the image would look at different screen resolutions – perfect for web design. (For more information on this, go to the **Hardware** chapter).

Previewing color accurately on text

If you are changing the color of text on an image you may have noticed that when you select your text there is a selection box around it. This selection box actually inverts the area it covers, making it very difficult to see what the color of your text looks like until it has been applied.

1

Press CTRL/CMD+H to hide the selection box. The text is still selected, but the selection is hidden.

You can now choose the Color Picker from the text Option bar and get a live preview of your color over the image you're working on.

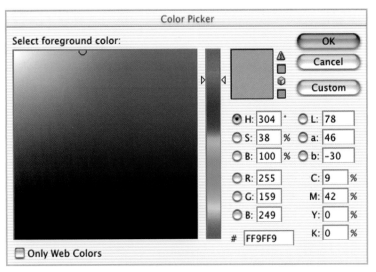

One very fast way to apply font styles is to select the text layer in the Layers palette. Click the name of the font in the text options bar. Use the up and down arrows to scroll through the fonts, or just go to the one you want. This also works for applying font sizes.

1

Using composites

One of the problems that Photoshop presents is that the image file sizes are often huge, and this can make work slow and laborious as you wait for images to load. Usually, you would want to open a PSD file with all the layers and channels visible, but sometimes speed is of the essence. If your image is very complex with lots of layers you may want to open a flattened version, as the smaller file size will make it faster to open.

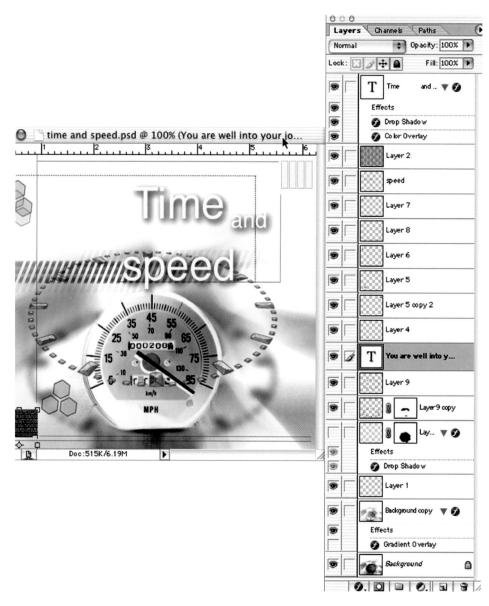

When opening your image via the **File > Open** dialog, hold down SHIFT+ALT while you click Open, and Photoshop will open a flattened version of your image. You'll see the following message - just click OK to continue.

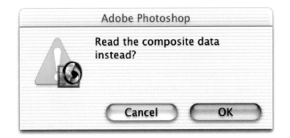

Here is the same image opened as a composite.

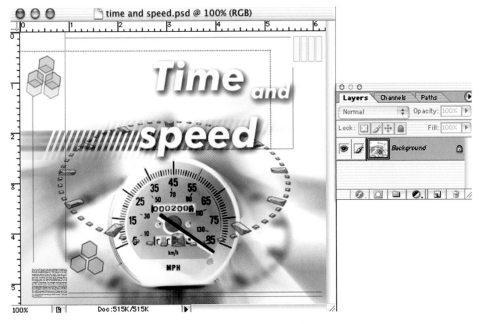

If you get a message saying that there is no composite available, it's because you haven't saved a composite image with your image. To fix this go to **Edit > Preferences > File Handling** and check **Always Maximize Compatibility for Photoshop (PSD) Files**. This option is usually turned on by default. The drawback of this is that it will increase the file sizes slightly, but if you are opening a lot of PSD files for viewing and converting then it's worth it.

1

Creating a composite layer

Have you ever wanted to make a layer that contains the content of all the layers without losing the individual layer information? This is called a composite layer.

1. Select the top layer.

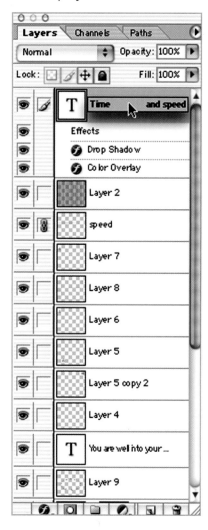

2. Create a new layer and name it composite. With this layer selected, go to the Layers palette, hold down the ALT key and select **Merge Visible**.

By holding the ALT key you have merged all the visible layers down, as you would expect, but only on this new layer. The rest of the image is left unaffected. Notice that all the layers remain intact and the thumbnail shows the contents of all the layers.

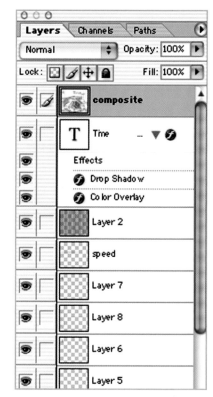

You could now apply an effect that will affect the entire image at once.

*If you wanted to make a composite of just a few of the layers only, then you would link these together first, then hold down ALT and select **Merge Linked**.*

Navigating images

Sometimes images are larger than can be displayed on your monitor and you can only see partial images, this is common when you zoom into an image. By using the navigator palette, you will see a red box around the portion of the image that is displayed in your window.

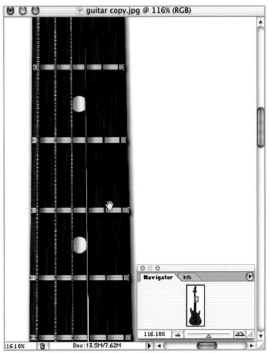

Click and drag the rectangle to navigate to a different part of your image.

You can also hold down the spacebar to temporarily choose the **Hand** tool and click and drag in your main image to navigate.

1

Navigation shortcuts

To jump to specific areas of a large image, use these keys

- Home: Top left corner

- End: Bottom right corner

- Page Down: One screen downwards

- Page Up: One screen upwards

Zooming in and out

Notice the two pictures of mountains in the bottom of the navigator palette.

Click on the larger mountains to zoom up on the image and the smaller mountains to zoom out.

- You can also zoom in and out of an image by pressing CTRL/CMD and the – and+ keys.

- Alternatively, enter a numerical percentage to quickly zoom. But remember that because of the nature of pixels and how they interact with the screen, an image will always display more accurately in increments of 25%.

- To enter a percentage and then be able to quickly change to another number, hold down SHIFT as you press ENTER. This way the percentage field is still highlighted, ready for you to enter a different number.

- You can also hold down CTRL/CMD and drag in the Navigator window to zoom in to a particular area.

- To show an image at 100% quickly, double-click the Zoom tool, or use the shortcut, CTRL/CMD+ALT+O.

- Press CTRL/CMD+0 to fit the entire image to the screen.

■ In other programs you may have used the shortcut CTRL/CMD+1 to view an image at actual size, in Photoshop, however this shortcut changes your view to look at only the Red channel. To get back to regular (RGB) view, press CTRL/CMD+~.

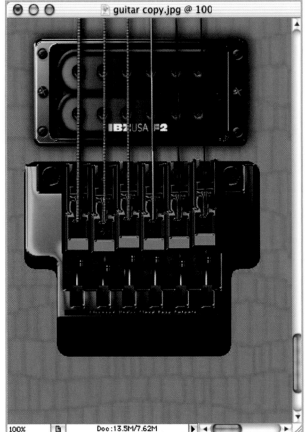

 To temporarily activate the Zoom tool while using any tool (other than the Type tool) press CTRL/CMD+SPACEBAR. Click (or click and drag) to zoom in and then let go of the keys to return to the tool you were using.

1

Drawing tricks

Quick on the draw

Ever tried to draw a circle in the center of a page?

1. Choose the Elliptical Marquee tool and the approximate center of the page.

2. If you hold down the ALT key as you drag out the ellipse, then it will take the center of the page as the center point of the ellipse. Hold down the SHIFT key to constrain to a perfect circle.

3. Fill with your color, by using these nifty shortcuts: ALT+ BACKSPACE to fill with color, and CTRL/CMD+ D to deselect.

4. Now comes the tricky part! What if we want to draw concentric circles? I played the guessing game for a while before I discovered this trick.

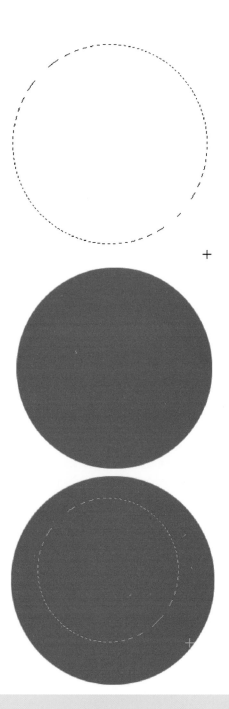

5. With the Elliptical Marquee tool, hold Shift (for a perfect circle), and begin to drag out your circle. Now press and hold the SPACEBAR. You can now move your entire selection while drawing it.

6. Once you have your selection centered, click the DELETE key to remove the center. CTRL/CMD+D to deselect.

See how easy it was to create a ring?

If you want complete accuracy you'll have to resort to snapping your selection to ruler lines, but if you don't need to be completely accurate, this is the fastest way to achieve this task.

If it's accuracy you're after, make sure under the View menu that Snap is checked. Then use CTRL/CMD+A to select the entire canvas. Drag out a horizontal and vertical ruler line – notice that they will snap to the center of the marquee. Because our marquee is the size of the entire canvas, we now have a crosshair showing us where the center of the canvas is. We can either ALT+SHIFT drag out our circle, or just SHIFT-drag to any size and move it so that it snaps to our crosshair. Concentric circles are now really easy as each one will snap to our crosshair.

1

Using the Transform Selection option

OK I've drawn an elliptical selection, what if I want to put it on an angle? Photoshop can't do that! Or can it?

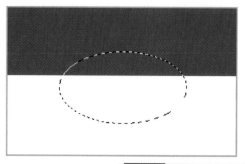

1. Fortunately Photoshop 7 boasts a great feature called Transform Selection. Go to **Select > Transform Selection**.

2. Now a bounding box will appear around the selection and you can transform it like any object.

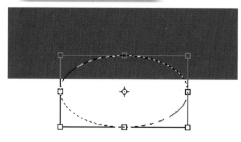

3. You can rotate it and move it.

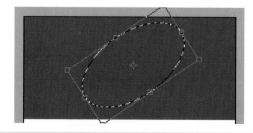

1

4. Just for fun, let's create one of those swishes that are so common on logos. Press ENTER to apply the transformation. Don't turn off the selection.

5. Press CTRL/CMD+SHIFT+I to inverse the selection. Press DELETE and we are left with our ellipse. Alternatively we could right/CTRL-click the selection and choose **Layer via Copy**.

6. Click CTRL/CMD+J to duplicate the ellipse layer and fill with white. Rotate and scale the top oval.

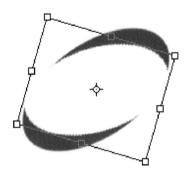 

A simple example, to show you what can be achieved with Transform Selection.

TRENDY LOGO

1

Aligning and distributing objects

When creating an interface, don't waste any time trying to line everything up, let Photoshop do the work for you.

1. First, link the layers that you want to align.

2. Select the Move tool, and take a look at the Options bar. You'll see two sets of buttons, on the right hand side of the bar. The ones on the left are the **Align** tools, and the ones on the far right are the **Distribute** tools. The icons are pretty self-explanatory.

3. Click the **Align top edges** button, and the top of the buttons will now become nicely aligned.

4. Then, from the Distribute buttons, select **Distribute to horizontal center**.

There! In two clicks, all the buttons are now perfectly arranged.

Free Transform

Let's have a look at a few transforming options that are right under our nose.

1. Press CTRL/CMD+T to enter Free Transform mode.

2. If you move the select tool over the corners or edges (8 resize nodes) you can scale the image. If you hold down the SHIFT key, it will scale proportionally.

3. When the Move tool is off a corner it will change to a curved, double sided arrow. Drag and you can rotate the image.

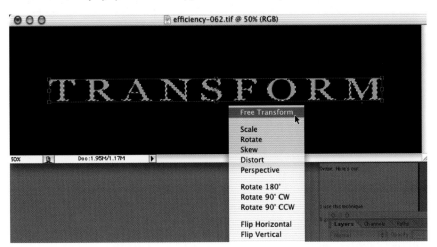

4. Right/CTRL-click and a popup menu will appear with more options.

5. Try the skew option. To do this in a controlled manner hold down the CTRL/CMD key and move nodes individually.

1

6. You can apply multiple transformations without applying effect. Here we have flipped horizontally and scaled the text.

You will have noticed that the Perspective and Distort options are grayed out. This is because the text can't be distorted in its current state. right/CTRL-click on the text layer's name in the Layers palette and choose **Rasterize Layer**. This will turn the text layer into a regular layer.

7. Now when you right/CTRL-click while in Free Transform mode, you'll see that all the options are available.

8. Choose Distort and see how you can now move each corner independently from the rest of the image.

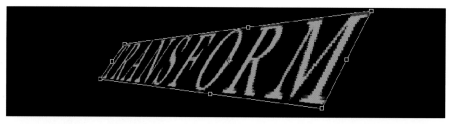

9. Experiment and you will find some fun and interesting variations.

Quality can suffer if you raster the type and make dramatic transformations. Instead, convert the type to a shape so it's still vector, transform, and then rasterize. Remember that once you rasterize, your text no longer will be editable, so bear in mind that you can also do a pretty good perspective effect, while still keeping the text editable using the Warp function in the options bar.

Crop it, but don't lose it

Have you ever cropped an image and then changed your mind? Here's a way to crop an image but not lose the edges, so you can make a late change.

1. Drag the crop tool out as usual.

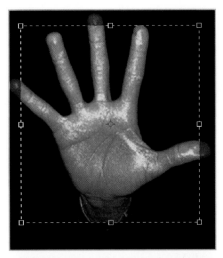

2. In the Options bar select **Hide** and **Shield**, rather than **Delete**. This will hide the cropped area instead of deleting it. In other words the canvas size will change, but the image won't be affected.

To make sure you don't crop out the wrong part of an image, select the areas you want to include in the image (hold down SHIFT and make simple Lasso selections). Then from the Image menu, choose Crop, and your image will be cropped as tightly as possible to these selected areas.

3. To apply crop quickly, double-click anywhere inside the cropping area or hit ENTER. Here's our image after cropping.

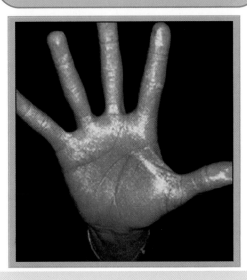

1

Notice we can pan the layer around and all the image data is still intact. You could use this technique to create an animated gif if you wanted.

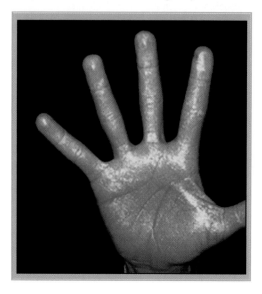 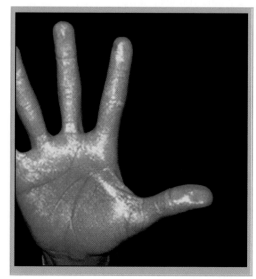

You can even scale the image down and make the entire original image fit in the window again.

You can also use the Crop tool in reverse – to add canvas size. Rather than using the Canvas Size command, simply increase the window size so that more gray area shows around the image. Drag with the Crop tool in the image. Then drag the corner handles outside the image, to visually add more canvas size.

1

Essential shortcuts

Every time you learn a new shortcut, your speed and efficiency is improved by 1.25 seconds – that's a definite infallible scientific fact. OK, it's not really – but you'll definitely see your work rate improve as you incorporate our favorite, "don't leave home without them" Photoshop shortcuts.

Tool shortcuts

Here are the common one-key keyboard shortcuts to select tools. Just press the corresponding key to select the tool. When there are two or more tools sharing the same spot in the toolbox (such as the Elliptical and Rectangular marquee tools), press SHIFT and the letter to switch tools.

Shortcut	Tool		Shortcut	Tool
M	Marquee		V	Move
L	Lasso		W	Magic Wand
C	Crop		K	Slice
J	Healing Brush		B	Paintbrush
S	Clone Stamp		Y	History Brush
E	Eraser		G	Gradient
R	Smudge		O	Sponge
A	Path Selection		T	Type
P	Path		U	Rectangle
N	Notes		I	Eyedropper
H	Hand		D	Default colors
X	Toggle colors		Q	Quick Mask mode
			F	Full screen mode

The best way to remember keyboard shortcuts is to use them frequently. There are keyboard shortcuts for just about everything you do in Photoshop. If you catch yourself doing an operation several times, as you work on a project, take a moment and look up the shortcut for it. Then practice it for the rest of that project. It might take a little longer at the start, but in the long run, you will save a lot of time.

1

Filling shortcuts

Let's look at a few shortcuts for filling objects and layers.

■ To fill with Background color, press CTRL/CMD+ BACKSPACE/DELETE.

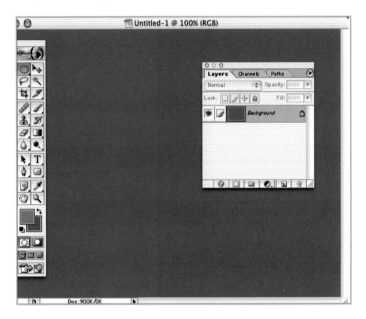

■ Create a layer and make a selection. Then fill with the Foreground color by pressing ALT+DELETE.

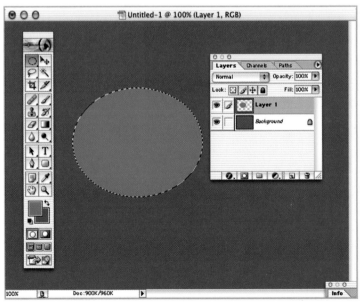

■ Deselect and then change the Foreground color.

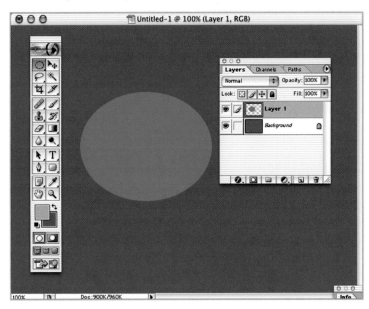

■ To fill all areas with pixel data and preserve transparency, press the SHIFT key in addition to the other shortcut. To fill with Foreground color, press SHIFT+ALT+DELETE.

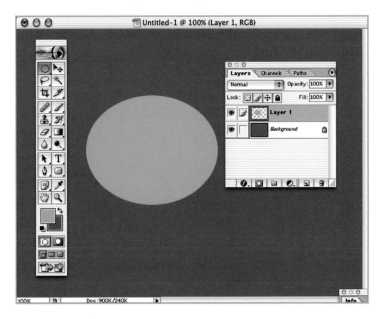

1

- To open the Fill dialog box press SHIFT+DELETE. In the dialog box you can choose a color or even a pattern.

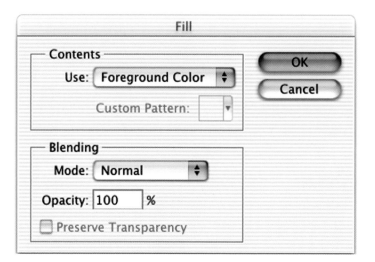

Repeating last filter

- To reapply a filter you have just used with exactly the same settings, just press the CTRL/CMD+F

- You can use this shortcut many times over to re-apply the filter to your taste.

- To use the same filter but change the settings, press CTRL/CMD+ ALT+F.

Recalling previous settings from a dialog box

Here is a simple shortcut that will take a lot of guesswork out of your work and save a lot of time. You can spend quite a lot of time getting the settings just right in a dialog box.

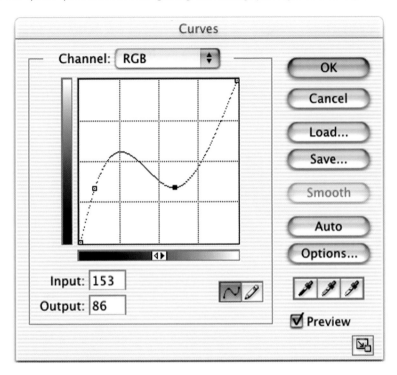

Usually when you reopen the dialog box all the settings are reset. If you hold down the ALT key when you launch a dialog box, it will recall the last used settings.

The key to efficiency in Photoshop is good preparation. Something as simple as naming your files clearly can save an enormous amount of time – particularly when deadlines are looming and your brain takes a quick holiday. Customizing tools and settings to suit your requirements again requires a certain amount of forward planning, but will speed up your work considerably. There are lots of tricks and shortcuts featured in this chapter - you may not memorize these all straight away, but the sooner you start incorporating them into your Photoshop work on a regular basis, the more streamlined your work will be.

Golden rules

Selection tools

Selection techniques

2: Selection secrets

Photoshop allows us to create new realities, to take our subject out of Birmingham and into the Bahamas without anyone being able to see the join. The key to this is making accurate selections, if you get it wrong then the results will be amateurish, but getting it right is rarely an easy task.

Many of us spend hours squinting over an image with the Lasso tool - in this chapter we'll cover the most efficient selection techniques, with plenty of tips and shortcuts thrown in. We'll also consider the idea that (as with so much in life) accurate Photoshop selections are all about looking at things from a fresh angle.

For example, in this image we want to select the mailbox:

What's the best way to do this? Use the Lasso to select around the outside of the mailbox, or perhaps the Magnetic Lasso to make things a little easier?

In fact, it is often much simpler (and quicker) to select the opposite of what you need – in this case the white background – and then inverse the selection so that the result is an appropriate selection.

2

Even the automated selection tools such as the Magic Wand rarely make a perfect selection with one click – you should be prepared to fine tune the selection so that, once again, your result is a great selection.

Think of all the selection options: Marquees, Lassos, and Magic Wand, as a toolkit, you're likely to dip in and out of your bag of tricks as you make your initial selection with one tool, and then fine-tune it with another.

Golden rules of selection

Before we go any further, let's consider a couple of the concepts crucial to making accurate selections. **Feathering** is an important aspect to get right simply because it is cumulative - you can only add to it, not reduce. Fine tuning is an essential part of the selection process.

Accurate feathering

Before using the Marquee or Lasso tools you need to think about the feather amount, specifically, you need to check the Options bar to see that the **Feather** value has been set appropriately.

The Options bar has a long memory, so if you previously set the Feather amount to a certain amount this value will remain there until you change it again. To ensure that you don't accidentally apply the wrong Feather value to a selection, keep the setting on the Options bar to zero, and instead right/CTRL-click in the selection to bring up a context sensitive menu.

Choose the feather amount and click OK. This way, you are adding the feathering you want, without changing the setting in the Options bar.

2

Using Quick Mask to preview feathering

It can be a challenge to determine how much feathering is the right amount for a selection. One method that can help is by taking advantage of Quick Mask mode to preview the amount of feathering. Here's how you do it:

- Make a selection with no feathering.

- Press Q to switch to Quick Mask mode, then use the Gaussian Blur filter to blur the mask.

This is the equivalent of feathering, with the added advantage that you can preview the end result, and, if necessary, adjust it.

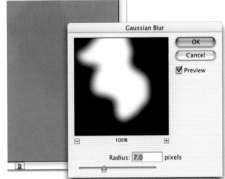

Fine-tuning selections

As mentioned previously, it is best to focus on the end result, rather than expecting to make a wonderful selection in one shot. We do this by fine tuning the selection, either adding to it or subtracting from it. There are two different ways to do this: by using the Options bar, or holding down keyboard combinations.

To add to an existing selection, click on the second button in the Options bar.

Or hold down SHIFT as you use a selection tool.

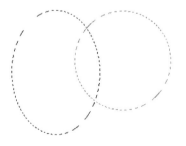
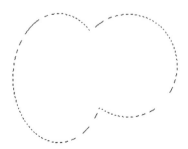

To remove from an existing selection, click on the third button in the Options bar:

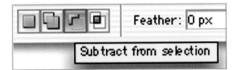

2

Or hold down ALT as you use a selection tool:

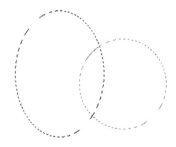

To create an intersection between the existing and new selections, click the fourth button in the Options bar:

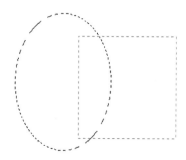

Or hold down SHIFT+ALT as you use a selection tool:

This concept works with any selection tools. It is possible (and often the best solution) to start with the Magic Wand and then switch to the Lasso, holding down SHIFT to add, or ALT to subtract from the selection.

Another method of fine tuning is through **Quick Mask**; we'll be looking at the Quick Mask in detail, later in the chapter.

Remember to undo

When making a selection, remember that you can use CTRL/CMD+Z to undo the last action. Also when using continuous selection tools like the Magnetic Lasso or the Lasso tool, bear in mind the fact that each time you click you place an anchor which locks that point down. These anchor points will save you a lot of work if you make a mistake right at the end of a selection. Click frequently, just like you save the file in progress frequently, to avoid time-consuming errors.

Selection tools

The Marquee tools

To use the Marquee tools more accurately, it is a good idea to fully exploit the settings in the Options bar: **Normal**, **Fixed Aspect Ratio**, or **Fixed Size**. As always with the Options bar, remember to check this setting each time before you use the Marquee tools.

Fixed Aspect Ratio allows you to preset the height:width ratio of your marquee.

Fixed Size marquees enable you to create a selection of a certain size - you'll find that when you select this option your Width and Height measurements will default to pixels.

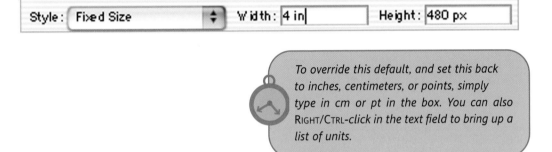

To override this default, and set this back to inches, centimeters, or points, simply type in cm or pt in the box. You can also RIGHT/CTRL-click in the text field to bring up a list of units.

Using the Spacebar to reposition as you select

Here's a trick that can be of great help in creating accurate marquee selections. As you are dragging to create a marquee selection, press the SPACEBAR, but don't release the mouse button. This will suspend the creation of the Marquee and let you drag to re-position it. Then let go of SPACEBAR to continue creating the Marquee. This is particularly useful when making elliptical or circular selections.

Making selections from the center outwards

Sometimes it is easier to create a marquee selection by drawing from the center outwards, rather than drawing from a corner. To do this, hold down ALT key as you drag with either Marquee tool and the marquee will be created from the center outwards.

2

The Lasso tools

Of the three Lasso tools: **Lasso**, **Magnetic Lasso**, and **Polygon Lasso**, the Lasso tool is the most manual since it creates selections where you click and drag (it's all up to you and your mousing skills!). The Magnetic Lasso attempts to find edges of contrast and snap to those edges, while the Polygon Lasso creates straight edged selections. It is unlikely that any one of these will create the exact selection that you want, so again, you should expect to swap tools as you do your fine tuning.

Using the Spacebar to scroll whilst selecting

It is common to zoom in a bit to get a closer view of the area that you are trying to select. However, as you get closer to the edge of your window, you may need to scroll your view to continue with your selection. Here's the dilemma: how to scroll the window without losing the selection you're in the middle of creating? The solution is the SPACEBAR. With any of the Lasso tools, hold down the SPACEBAR to interrupt the Lasso and get the Hand tool. Click and drag to scroll to the view you want, and then let go of the SPACEBAR to continue with your selection. The pointer will continue where you last left off.

> Be careful not to move the mouse when you release the SPACEBAR, especially with a movement sensitive tool like the Magnetic Lasso, the results may be quite surprising.

The Lasso tool and the Alt key

As a general rule, when using the Lasso tool, always hold down ALT when you are creating a new selection. There are two reasons for doing this. First, if you let go of the mouse buttons without any key held down, the Lasso tool thinks you're finished, and closes off the selection. By holding down ALT, you can let go of the mouse, re-position it, etc., and the selection will not close off. Second, if you are using the Magnetic Lasso tool and want to switch on the fly to the Lasso or Polygon Lasso tool, the ALT key does this too. With this key held down, click and drag to make the Magnetic Lasso behave as the Lasso, single click and it will act as the Polygon Lasso. Release ALT to use the Magnetic Lasso.

The Magic Wand tool

The Magic Wand is a useful tool, but it is unlikely to make a perfect selection with one click – in fact, many people spend way too much time trying over and over with different tolerance settings, trying to get the perfect selection. Instead, try this technique: use a lower tolerance setting and use the SHIFT key to add to the existing selection. If you add a little too much to the selection, fix it later using one of the fine tuning methods described below.

Using the Eyedropper to improve performance

Believe it or not, the setting for the Eyedropper tool plays an important role in the performance of the Magic Wand. In the first example, the Eyedropper tool option was set to Point sample. With a Tolerance of 15, a large area of the sky was selected.

Then, the Eyedropper setting was changed to 5 by 5 average. Using the same tolerance setting of 15 and clicking on the same spot (using the guides), a much larger area was selected.

Basically, if you're not getting the results you want, try changing the Eyedropper settings before using the Magic Wand.

You can use Tool Presets to create a variety of tolerance settings. Then just pick from a tool preset, rather than typing in different tolerance settings.

Pen tools

The **Pen** tools can also act as selection tools, offering a couple of important advantages. First, compared with selection edges, it is very easy to adjust the path that is created by the Pen tool. Second, the path can be saved as part of the image. The saved path adds very little to the file size, yet saves the selection information in the document.

Adding and deleting anchor points

Rather than switching between the Pen tool and the **Add Anchor** or **Delete Anchor** point tools, just stick with the Pen tool. To add an anchor point, position your mouse on the path where no anchor point exists (look for a plus sign beside the Pen icon). Click to add a point. To delete an anchor, position the Pen over an existing anchor point (look for a minus sign beside the Pen icon). Click to remove a point.

It's a good idea to be zoomed in nice and close when deleting anchor points, otherwise you risk missing the anchor point, and instead of deleting it, you end up creating a really funky path! Always remember that you can fall back on the good ol' CMD/CTRL+Z to undo any disasters.

Converting anchor points

Exactly the same concept applies when converting anchor points - don't switch to the **Convert Point** tool, simply keep hold of the Pen tool and hold down ALT. Click on a curved anchor point to convert to a straight point. To convert a straight point to a curved point, keep holding down ALT and then drag outwards to create handles for the bezier curve.

While using the Pen tool you can create the curves on the fly. Simply place a point then click and drag the next point – this will automatically take you into curve editing and shape the line you've just made.

2

Editing anchor points

To use the **Direct Selection** tool to move and edit anchor points, keep the Pen tool as your active tool and hold down CTRL/CMD. When you want to use the Pen tool again, just let go of CTRL/CMD.

Scaling a path

If you've created a path and you need to make it slightly larger or smaller overall, don't edit the individual anchor points. To scale the overall path, use the Selection tool and in the Options bar, check **Show Bounding Box**.

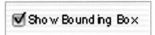

Then use the handles to scale the path. Press ENTER to finalize the transformation.

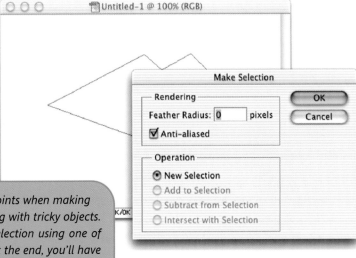

Making a selection from a path

To make a selection based on the path press CTRL/CMD+RETURN. Or CTRL/CMD and click on the path name. To add options such as feathering, hold down ALT and click on the **Load Path as Selection** button in the Paths palette.

Remember to place frequent anchor points when making your selections, especially when working with tricky objects. If you've been working on a twisted selection using one of the Lasso tools, and then screw it up at the end, you'll have to do the whole lot over again, unless you slap down a bunch of intermittent points in the process.

2

The Select menu

There are many options available under the Select menu that can help to alter, enhance, or fine tune selections. Here are some of the key functions and how to take advantage of them.

Color Range

When you need to select areas based on colors, you can use the Magic Wand, or, for a more interactive technique, go to **Select > Color Range**. Pick the color you want to select, and then use the Fuzziness slider to adjust the selection. To fine tune the selection, use the eyedroppers to add to or subtract from the selection. You can preview your selected area in various ways, including Grayscale, Black Matte, and White Matte, as shown here, or Quick Mask.

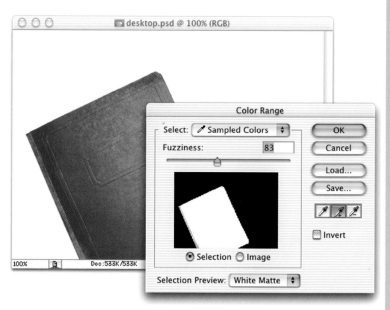

You may come across problems when using the Color Range option if your chosen color appears in more than one spot. To overcome this, use the Marquee tool to mark out your desired area first. A pre-selection selection, if you like.

Don't worry about accuracy, here – just try to separate the areas where the similar colors exist.

Once we have this area selected we can also use the **Add to Sample** button (just to the right of the color picker), which helps to select colors that are outside our fuzziness range. Fuzziness only applies to our current hue. Sometimes however, completely different hues creep into the area whose color we're trying to change, so adding these to our selection is really useful.

Modify

The **Modify** commands can adjust a selection in a variety of ways. Let's take the selection shown below and experiment with each option to see what they do.

Border: converts the selection into a border or frame selection

Here, a new layer was created, the border selection was filled, and the ripple filter applied.

Smooth: Checks around each selected pixel to find any unselected pixels based on the value you add. Use this to add more pixels to a selection while making the edge smoother.

Expand: makes the selection larger based on a value you enter while keeping the basic shape of the selection.

2

In this example, a new layer was created, the expanded selection was filled, and several motion blur filters were applied.

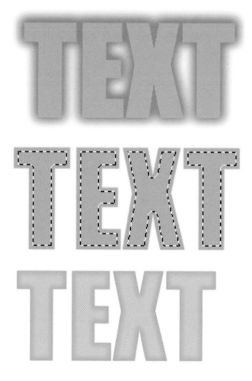

Contract: makes the selection smaller based on the value you enter while keeping the basic shape of the selection.

Here, a new layer was added, the selection was filled with a lighter version of the original color, and a blur filter was applied.

Grow

Here's a useful command when you've made a selection and it's not quite what you need. For example, you've used the Magic Wand but the tolerance wasn't quite high enough.

Rather than changing the tolerance or adding to the selection, you can also right/CTRL-click, or go to **Select > Grow**. Each time you choose this command the selection will grow contiguously. In other words the selection will expand to encompass pixels that are a bit further away from the stated tolerance, but still adjacent to the original selection.

2

Similar

A similar concept to Grow, this command will select areas that are similar to the current selection. By nature, the **Similar** command selects pixels throughout the entire image, as opposed to contiguously. To access the command, you can right/CTRL-click, or choose it from the Select menu.

> *The range of pixels selected by both these commands is determined by the Tolerance setting of the Magic Wand*

Transform Selection

Use this command to add handles to your selection to transform it.

- Click and drag on any handle to scale the selection – use SHIFT to scale proportionally

- To rotate the selection, move your mouse just outside the handles until you see a rotate symbol, then drag to rotate

- You can click and drag the center point to any of the anchor points on the bounding box, and the rotation will center on that point

Hold down:

- ALT to transform from the center outwards

- SHIFT to transform proportionally

- CTRL/CMD to edit each handle independently.

- Right/CTRL-click to pop up a menu of choices, including **Skew**, **Distort**, and **Perspective**.

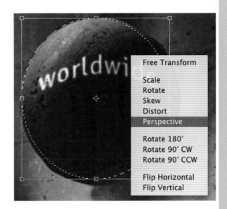

> *To apply a transformation click ENTER. To cancel a transformation hit the ESC key on your keyboard.*

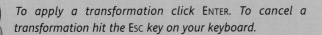

2

Save Selection

Saving a selection as an Alpha Channel

To avoid having to make a complex selection more than once, you can save a selection as an **Alpha Channel**. An Alpha Channel is an additional channel that is added to the Channels palette that stores selection information for later use

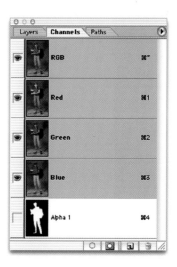

To create a channel, make a selection and then from the Select menu, choose Save Selection – you can name the channel if you wish.

Click on the channel in the Channels palette, and you'll see your selection represented by shades of gray. White pixels represent the selected area; black pixels are the areas that are not selected, while gray areas represent partial (feathered) selections.

Channel shortcuts

- To load the channel as a selection, choose **Select > Load Selection**, or CTRL/CMD+click on the channel

- To load the channel and add to an existing selection, hold down CTRL/CMD+SHIFT and click on the channel

- To load the channel and subtract from an existing selection, hold down CTRL/CMD+ALT and click on the channel

- To load the channel and intersect with an existing selection, hold down CTRL/CMD+SHIFT+ALT and click on the channel

2

Viewing channels as Quick Masks

To assist in editing an Alpha Channel, it might help to look at it as if you are in Quick Mask mode. To do this, in the Channels palette, click on the Alpha Channel to view it, and then click on the eyeball beside the RGB channel.

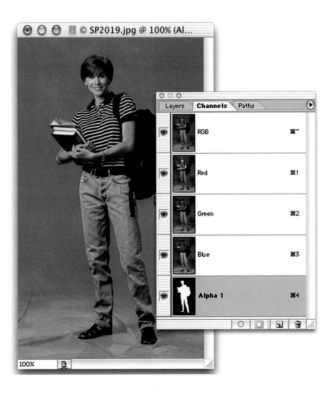

Selection techniques

2

Quick Mask

Quick Mask offers some distinct advantages over other selection methods:

- You can see the effects of feathering.

- It is possible to apply filters and finer detail work to your selection.

- You can view your selection as a colored overlay, rather than surrounded by marching ants.

- To fine tune a selection in Quick Mask mode, just remember that black is the masking color, meaning that you should paint with black any areas that you do not wish to be selected. These areas will be represented by the colored overlay.

- To add areas to the selection, paint with white.

- The brush you use has an important impact in Quick Mask: a soft edged brush will created feathered selections, while hard edged brushes create a selection with no feathering.

Quick Mask keyboard shortcuts

- Press Q to move in and out of Quick Mask mode

- Press X to swap between black and white as the foreground color

- Press [(left bracket) to make the brush size smaller, press] (right bracket) to make the brush size larger

Using Quick Mask to adjust a selection

It's common to create a selection that is almost perfect, but not quite tight enough, or to create a good selection, and then decide that you want to expand it to include a slight border.

Theoretically, you could use the **Modify** command and **Expand** or **Contract** the selection. Unfortunately, you may not know exactly what number to enter to get the desired result. Here's how Quick Mask can help once again.

In Quick Mask mode, you can go to **Filter > Other > Maximum** to make the selection larger.

Alternatively, you could select **Filter > Other > Minimum** to make the selection smaller. Take advantage of the filter preview to determine the appropriate amount to enter to get the result you want.

Using Quick Mask to create border effects

Follow these simple steps to get a weird and wonderful selection that will make a great border edge.

1. Make a rectangular selection leaving a small border around the outside (you can also make a more unusual selection as shown here).

2

2. Hit Q to go into Quick Mask mode (press Q)

3. From the Filter menu, apply one or more filters such as Brush Strokes; Spatter and other distort filters (avoid filters that add or create anything such as Render Clouds).

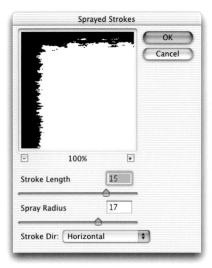

4. Press Q to return to Regular mode, and then use the selection to create a border (you can do this in a number of ways, perhaps most easily by adding a Layer Mask, or creating a new layer and filling with white).

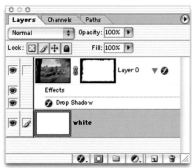

Using Quick Mask to create rounded corners

Photoshop has some vector drawing tools in the form of the shape tools, but there are limits to how much you can really do with these tools. A hidden feature of Quick Mask is the ability to take a feathered selection and remove the feathering while leaving the rounded corners. Here's how to take advantage of this to create unusual shapes with rounded corners.

1. Create a series of Marquee selections that overlap (hold down SHIFT to add to the selection).

2. Right/CTRL-click and choose Feather. Add a feather of 6 – 8 pixels.

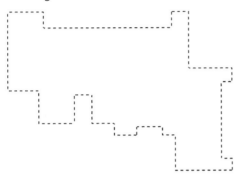 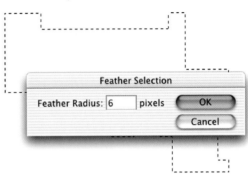

3. Switch to Quick Mask mode (press Q).

4. From the **Image** menu, choose **Adjustments > Brightness/Contrast**. Change the Contrast to around 96 until you see the feathering turning sharp. Click OK.

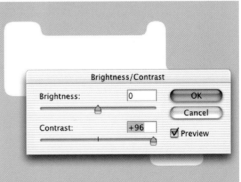

2

5. Create a new layer and fill with a color. Add layer styles as requested.

Extract

To access the **Extract** command, (which used to live under the Image menu in Photoshop 6) go to **Filter > Extract**. A separate dialog box will open with specialized tools and commands. The idea here is that you use the **Edge Highlighter** tool to define the edges of the object you wish to keep, and then use the **Fill** tool to paint in the rest of the desired area. Use a small highlighter brush for sharp edges, and larger brush sizes for areas with detail such as hair.

It is also very effective for fast masking of a large area for later fine tuning.

The **Preview** button lets you see the results, and if necessary, use the **Edge Touchup** and **Cleanup** tools to fine tune the edge.

When dealing with an image with sharp edges, it is important to follow the edge as closely as possible using a small brush size. The **Smart Highlighting** option can help with this process. Check the box and the brush will snap to contrasting edges. Alternatively you could leave this option unchecked and simply hold down CTRL/CMD to activate Smart Highlighting whenever you need it.

2

Using Extract for border effects

Here's a quick way to employ the Extract command to create a funky border effect.

1. Use the Highlight tool to create a series of lines. If you want the lines to be straight remember to hold down the SHIFT key as you draw them.

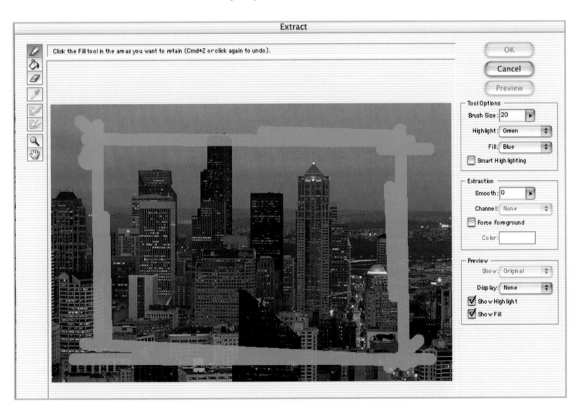

2

2. Fill the middle with the Fill tool.

3. Click OK, and there you have it - a nifty edge effect.

Remember, the Background layer is converted to a regular layer and the outside pixels are erased to transparent, so for this tip it's best to work on a copy of the image.

Using the History Brush with the Extract tool

No matter how perfectly you paint around an image in the extract dialog box, there are times when there will be parts of an image missing once extracted.

Take a look at the beak, there's a nasty gap in it now. How would you go about fixing this? Would you use a Paintbrush and paint the missing parts back into the image? Or perhaps use the Rubber Stamp tool? Maybe you would make a new layer with the entire image and cut and paste a selection. Well, these are good solutions, but there is a much speedier way to fix this problem, and it comes in the guise of the **History brush**.

1. This History brush will paint from a previous history state into your image; let's try it out now. Start by selecting the brush from the Tools palette.

2. In the History palette, click to the left of the state before the **Extract** stage. This will target this state of the image as the snapshot for the History brush.

2

3. Choose a small hard-edged brush. A soft brush would not give a solid enough definition to the edge.

4. Begin to paint over the image and notice all the lost detail comes back, just like new.

Removing matting

Sometimes when you cut out an image you will see dark edges left over.

The quick way to fix this is to select the layer with the image on it, go to **Layer > Matting > Remove Black Matte**.

The edges are cleaned up automatically. Naturally, if you are working with an image on a dark background you may see a light edge. You can fix this by choosing **Remove White Matte** instead of black.

Background Eraser

The Background Eraser can be used to change portions of an image to transparent, leaving you with a separate layer. Here's a lightning speed checklist to using the tool effectively.

- Change the Sampling setting from Continuous to Once.

- Lower the Tolerance setting from 50% to a lower setting such as 30%.

- Check the **Protect Foreground Color** box. Hold down the ALT key and click on the color you don't want to erase.

Click on the color you want to erase, and start painting.

2

■ To get a vivid idea of how the tool is working it helps to add a new layer below and fill it with a contrasting color.

■ Remember, the Background Eraser automatically changes the Background Layer to Layer 0, so you may want to make a backup copy of a document before using this tool.

Channel selection

Sometimes all the traditional selection methods just don't work — particularly in cases where you have fine edges to select (such as hair or blades of grass). One approach that often helps is to start in the **Channels** palette.

Using Channels to make selections

When you make a selection and then go to **Select > Save Selection**, an Alpha Channel will automatically be created. That channel is made up of white (the selection) and black (the mask, or non-selected areas). Here, we're going to take the opposite approach, to create a channel that will become a selection.

1. With an RGB image open, go to the Channels and look at each of the channels (Red, Green and Blue). Pick the one that gives you the best start towards creating a black and white mask (focus your attention on the challenge – in this case the grass against the background).

2. Duplicate the channel and make sure you work on the copy; else you'll ruin your image. Then use the **Levels** command (CTRL/CMD+L) to make the light areas whiter and the dark areas blacker.

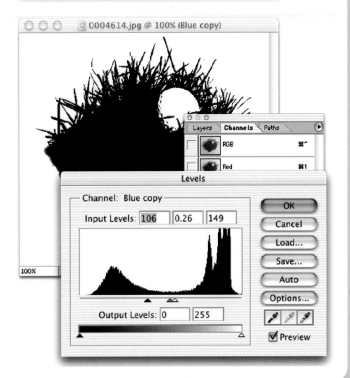

2

3. Do any touch-ups by painting areas with black and white paint. Your final result should be a black and white mask.

4. Load the channel as a selection, by either going to **Select > Load Selection**, or CTRL/CMD-click on the Alpha Channel). If necessary, fine tune the selection.

Here, the selection was used to separate the grass onto a separate layer.

> It's a good idea to add a Gaussian blur of 0.5 to 1.0 pixels, prior to saving the channel; this will eliminate some of the hard edges.

> To load the highlight areas or shadows of an image as a selection, press CTRL/CMD+ALT+~. You can then invert the selection by pressing CTRL/CMD+SHIFT+I.

Adjustment Layers

Using Adjustment Layers to help with selection

No matter how accomplished you become with various selection tools, you may well encounter images that present a definite challenge such as this intimidating character.

We're trying to select his arm, but the image is so over-exposed that it is very difficult to distinguish between this area and the one behind it. Certainly an automatic tool such as the Magic Wand is not going to be much help, since there's no real contrast for the tool to work with.

Here's a great trick that is perfect for this, and many other challenging situations.

1. Add an Adjustment Layer – could be Levels, Hue/Saturation or Curves. The aim is to adjust the image with only one goal in mind: creating some contrast in the challenging area, the doctor's arm. Don't worry about the rest of the image for now.

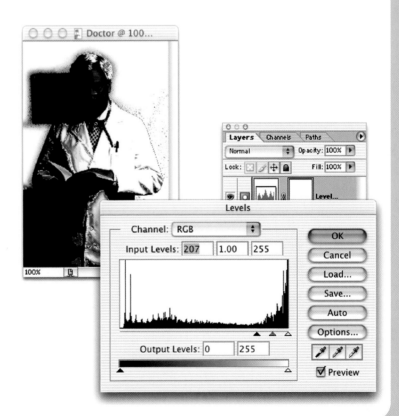

2

2. Once you have a good contrast, click OK and use whatever tools you wish to make the selection. If you are using the Magic Wand tool, then check the **Use All Layers** box in the Options bar. Only work on the challenging area – you can add to the selection in a moment.

3. Now delete the Adjustment Layer to return to the original image. If necessary, fine tune the remainder of the selection.

Layer based selections

As soon as you put anything on a layer by itself, it is, in effect, selected. You can easily load a layer as a selection by CTRL/CMD-clicking on its name in the Layers palette. You can use this as an on-going selection technique – put something on a layer in order to select it. You can use techniques such as the Background Eraser, Extract or other selection techniques to separate elements onto a separate layer.

Finding the center of objects on a layer

If you need to find the center of an object that's on a layer, here's a simple method.

1. Make sure you have the Rulers showing (CTRL/CMD+R). Then press CTRL/CMD+T to bring up the Free Transform command.

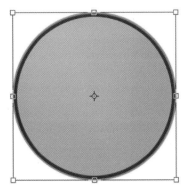

2. Click on the vertical ruler and drag a guide onto the center point in Free Transform, it should snap to the center point. Repeat with the horizontal ruler to add a second guide.

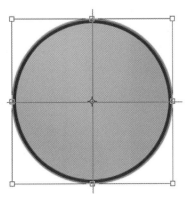

3. Press Esc to get out of Free Transform.

2

When Defringe doesn't work

The Defringe command (**Layer > Matting > Defringe**) is designed to deal with the small fringe of color that sometimes shows around the outside of a newly created layer.

Unfortunately, it doesn't always fix the problem, but here's a technique that can help.

1. CTRL/CMD click on the layer name to load it as a selection, then go to **Select > Modify > Contract**, for the Contract Selection use a value of 1 or 2.

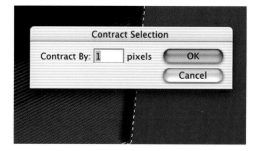

2. Inverse the selection, by clicking CTRL/CMD+SHIFT+I.

3. Use the Gaussian Blur filter to apply a very slight blur. You may want to hide the selection edges to make it easier to see the effect. (**View > Show > Selection Edges**, or CTRL/CMD+H).

The secret to success in Photoshop is undoubtedly the ability to make neat, accurate selections. And the key to mastering selections is to know the best shortcuts: the ones that help you make changes on the fly, and the hidden features that allow you to make more intuitive selections. The golden rule is to always focus on the desired end result, and use a combination of tools and features to achieve it

2

3: Layers

Working with layers is one of the greatest things in Photoshop, and the ability to manipulate individual sections to create an image has been a blessing since the early days. But there are so many things you can do with them that a lot of time is spent creating, duplicating, and manipulating layers. Here are a few tips and tricks to aid and speed up your work.

Layer basics

Creating a layer

The fastest way to create a new layer is to click on the icon on the Layers palette. This would be a good method to use if you just want a blank layer sitting by itself above your currently selected layer.

If you press ALT when clicking this icon, then it will bring up the New Layer dialog box, which we normally see when we create a layer via the **Layer > New > Layer** route or by using the CTRL/CMD+SHIFT+N shortcut.

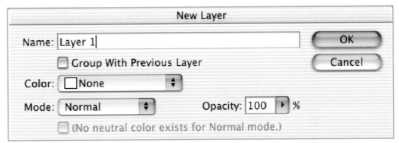

This allows us to name the layer, and adjust its mode and opacity right from the outset: speed and functionality.

To create a new layer below the current layer, (as long as it is not the Background layer), hold down CTRL/CMD as you click on the new layer icon.

Duplicating a layer for effect

1. Here's a quick and easy method to create a text shadow effect. First create some text (in my example I used the word Photoshop), and then duplicate this layer in one of the following ways:

- Go to **Layer > Duplicate Layer**.

- Or right/CTRL-click on the layer in the Layers palette, and select **Duplicate Layer**.

- Click CTRL/CMD+J to automatically create a copy of the active layer.

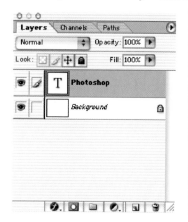 

2. Rasterize your duplicate text layer – by going to **Layer > Rasterize > Type**. You are now free to add effects or transform at will.

3. With the duplicate layer selected, click CTRL/CMD+T to access Free Transform mode, and now skew and distort the text as you please. When you're happy with your changes, hit the big check mark in the right hand corner of the Options bar to confirm your transformation.

4. Either feather it 2-4 pixels, or add a Gaussian Blur of about 2-4 pixels. Then click SHIFT+CTRL/CMD+I to select inverse, and hit DELETE. Drop the opacity of the layer to about 50%. Voila! A simple shadow effect.

This method also works on selections of a layer. Choose your selection, and click leaving the original layer completely intact. In this example, I've selected three sections of my main text layer. I then clicked CTRL/CMD+J so that my selections were copied onto their own layers. On each of the three new layers I added a motion blur, and reduced the opacity to get the fading effect, and finally added a layer style for the original text layer:

3

Centering a layer

You can copy a layer from one picture to another simply by clicking in the Layers palette and dragging the layer from image 1 over to image 2. As you let go of the button, the new layer will automatically be added to the second image. Hold down the SHIFT key as you release the button, to center the new layer.

At times this SHIFT-drag method just isn't suitable, so here's a canny trick to center any object accurately centered on another layer.

1. With your image open, click SHIFT+CTRL/CMD+N to create a brand new layer, and give it a memorable name – I've called mine 'CenterBar'.

2. With this layer selected, click U to select the Line tool, and in the Options bar select a 2 pixel weight.

3. Using the Info tab (use **Window > Info** to open the palette if needed) draw a simple line from the 0,0 point of your image document to the bottom most point of your image.

3

4. Now paste your new object into its own layer, and name this layer, too. I called mine 'newstuff'. Arrange the layer so that it sits directly under the Centerbar layer.

5. Select the Centerbar layer and click next to the eyeball icon to link it to the newstuff layer.

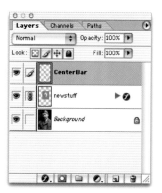

6. Choose the **Move** tool (V) and take a look at the alignment tools on the Options bar, click once on the **Horizontal Alignment** tool and once on the **Vertical Alignment** tool and your object will be perfectly centered in the new layer. You can now delete the CenterBar layer, or hide it for later use.

Due to the straight line going through the picture diagonally, this method will always center your object, regardless of how many layers or the shape of other layers or objects you work with. The good thing about this trick is it can be used on any image, as many times as you want.

Loading a layer as a selection

There is a really easy way to load a layer as a selection. If we wanted to select the ring in this picture:

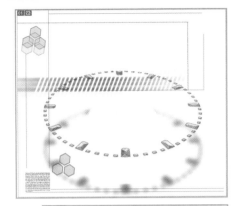

3

Find the layer and CTRL/CMD+click on the layer thumbnail...

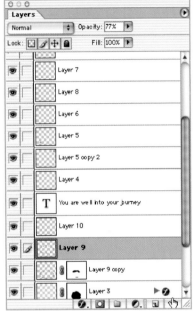

...and the "marching ants" will appear, indicating the layer is selected.

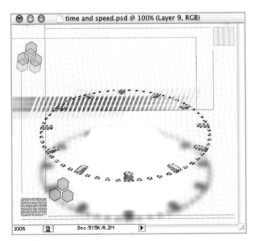

3

Creating new documents from layers

Look at the collage below, the aim here is to take a layer from the image and to create a new document with it. To achieve this you could hide and delete all the other layers, before renaming the document, but it is quicker if you use the following method:

1. Select the layer you want to use.

2. In the fly-out Layers palette menu, select **Duplicate Layer**.

3. In the dialog that appears, choose **New** as the destination document.

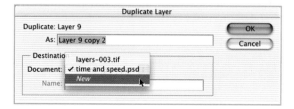

A new document will be created with our layer on it.

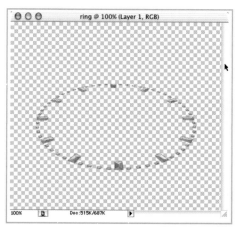

Managing layers

Name your layers!

Using layers gives us real freedom to explore creative ideas in Photoshop, but have you ever been working away, and then realized that you have created 8 billion layers and you can't remember which one is which? Sometimes a thumbnail just isn't enough to go on. To rename a layer, all you need to do is double-click the name it currently has. Remember, double-clicking the icon of the layer brings up the Layer Style options.

3

Deleting hidden layers

I almost jumped for joy when I beta tested Photoshop 7 and discovered that it had a feature to delete the hidden layers. My style of work involves many layers, so I used to spend ages dragging the unused ones to the trash.

Here is a typical Layers palette with a few hidden layers that need to be deleted.

Make sure that all of the layers you wish to keep are showing, (with the handy eyeball icon displayed to confirm their visibility). This is extremely important; all hidden layers will be deleted, so if you're not careful you could lose some of your useful layers.

Check your layer sets too, to make sure that you don't have any hidden layers there that you wish to keep. If an entire Layer set is hidden, then the whole lot will be deleted.

Then open the fly out menu from the top corner of the Layers palette and select **Delete Hidden Layers**. Photoshop will now do all the housework for you.

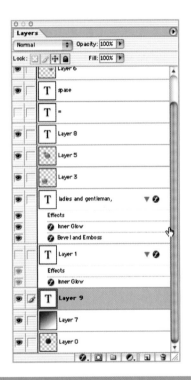

Using the Layer controls

Sometimes you might want to change the color of something. Seems easy enough. But what if the object has a faded edge?

3

What if we want to make the blurry sphere blue? If we just use the paint bucket and click inside the sphere we get this:

Not a very good rendition! We could adjust the hue/saturation of the layer, or add an adjustment layer, or even use a Color Overlay from the layer styles options. But what if we want to use a very specific blue? That's difficult to get right. Here's a quick way of doing this.

Let's lock the transparency of the layer by clicking on the **Lock transparent pixels** tab, in the top left of the Layers palette.

To quickly turn Lock transparent pixels on and off, press /

Locking transparent pixels means that only the opaque areas of the layer can be manipulated. Now we can just fill the layer with the blue we desire. And our fade is nicely preserved.

Locking transparent pixels can be both a help and a hindrance when using filters. For example, to Add Noise to only the pixels on a layer, transparent pixels should be locked. If however, you're trying to apply a Gaussian Blur to the edges of those pixels, the filter will not work if the lock command is turned on.

We've seen how **Lock transparent pixels** will allow us to seamlessly recolor the layer, but how would we use the other Layers palette locks?

- **Lock image pixels** can be used to move an image around its layer without accidentally modifying it.

- **Lock position** will lock the layer so that it can still be modified, but not moved around.

- **Lock all** allows us to lock the layer entirely so that it can't be altered at all.

Clipping groups

Using clipping groups to create effects

The real power of layers lies in combining them creatively: Take a look at this image, how would you go about making it?

3

You could use the Marquee tool to create the J shape, or perhaps use a mask. But what if we wanted a little more flexibility? Even with masks, if we wanted to change the J to another letter or shape there'd be a lot of extra work involved.

1. To recreate this picture, type a huge letter in whichever font you choose.

2. Add a layer with the picture you want to inlay just above your text layer.

3. With this new layer selected, click CTRL/CMD+G to group with the previous layer. Doing things this way keeps our font intact – it's still text, which means we can change it at any time.

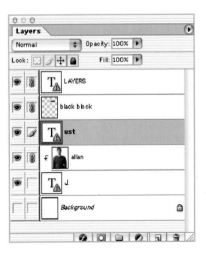

> *You can also group two layers together by pressing ALT whilst hovering between the two layers that you wish to group – when you see the little group icon appear, click and the layers will be grouped. You can un-group two layers in the same way.*

3

So the image is using the layer below as a **Layer Clipping Group**: the pixels on the bottom layer (the J) clip the layers above. This technique will also work with multiple layers. Whatever is opaque on the layer below will be used as a guide as to what should be displayed on the layer above. Everything that falls outside this area will not be displayed.

Linking all these layers together (as shown in the image above) means we can move the entire composite image around together. It's an autonomous unit, so we can change its components at any time without much fuss.

This can be particularly useful when you are working in a volatile environment such as web development. Clients often change their minds at the last moment and it's important to use techniques that save precious time.

Use a clipping group to avoid rasterizing type

To apply a filter to type you normally have to rasterize the type. With this trick you can create a fill effect using filters, without having to rasterize your type. Create a new layer above the type, fill it and apply a filter such as Texturizer. Then press CTRL/CMD+G to **Group with Previous**, and it will look as though the type has a filter applied – but the text is still editable.

Of course, this method has limitations; the edges of the text cannot be modified in this way.

Blending Modes

Blending modes are so called because they **blend** two or more layers together. Always keep in mind that the effect you're creating with these modes is a composite one – both layers create the effect.

Blending modes in action

So how do we know which blending modes to use, and when to use them? There are five main groups that blending modes are divided into. By way of introducing them and demonstrating a useful way to use each, let's look at a practical example to illustrate a good way to use these modes.

Here's our picture without any modification.

Let's say our task is to soften the image and give the model a healthy glow. The lighting in the image is pretty stark, giving the image a harsh, flat appearance.

What we'd like to do first is get a bit of depth going in the image. The harsh lighting is pretty uniform, flattening the visual plane. But how do we bring out the light and dark areas? Ideally, we'd like to start by isolating the light areas. We'll use the **Burn** blending modes to achieve this, as we're hoping to compound the effects onto our background layer.

Burning

3

The Burn blending modes affect the darker half of the palette colors, emphasizing the black area of the image, they include **Darken**, **Multiply**, **Color Burn**, and **Linear Burn.**

Our final plan here is to use the **Screen** blending mode, which will drop out all the dark areas. Seems a funny way to go about it: we're actually *creating* dark areas at the moment! Have a look at the original picture again. Where are the really light areas? They are mostly on the girl's face, but there is also a lot of light on the background wall.

We want to isolate these areas so that we can use them for our Screen. By isolating these areas and then using a Screen blending mode we will make these areas more prominent. This will help with our visual depth problem: As light strikes an object, the parts of the object that are closest to the camera are brighter, and as we move further away the object is darker. Obviously if the object is flat the light is uniform.

By making the light areas even lighter we are helping to create the illusion of depth – contrasting light would mean greater changes in the surface plane. To achieve this we want to darken everything except the lightest areas. When we use our Screen blending mode, all but the lightest areas will fall away.

Keep in mind that because we are blending to the original, with a combination of light and dark areas, the original light areas are preserved. If we were blending onto a layer of flat dark grey – *all* the areas, *including* the light areas would become darker. Let's demonstrate this:

In this example I have duplicated the background layer, and then desaturated this duplicate, by going to **Image > Adjustments > Desaturate**.

After pumping up the contrast a bit, I posterized the image - **Image > Adjustments > Posterize**, and then used a cutout to drop the complexity of the line **Filter > Artistic > Cutout**.

3

This gives us some indication of the areas that are going to glow with our final result. Now let's see what happens if we change the blending mode of this duplicate layer to Multipy.

Notice how all the dark areas belong to the cutout image, but all the lighter ones are from the original picture. That's because the light areas of the cutout image have become transparent while the darker areas are opaque – which to a (rather primitive) degree sums up how burn blending modes work.

Ok demonstration over, back to our task at hand. We're using the Color Burn mode in the classic sense – to drop out all the light areas. So the light areas of our original image underneath show through, and the darker areas are compounded. So here you can see the duplicated layer, (without any filters or posterization this time) using the Color Burn mode.

Dodging

We now need to create a merged layer. Create a new layer, and then hit CTRL/CMD+A to select the entire canvas, then go to **Edit > Copy Merged**, and paste into the new layer.

This basically copies everything that we can see to a new layer without affecting the original layers.

You can see that the new merged layer actually *looks* burnt. The new merged layer has all of the effects applied, but has no actual blending modes applied to it anymore, and can now be used with new blending modes, which is what we will do shortly.

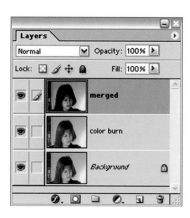

We can now turn our color burn layer off, as we won't be using it anymore. Let's Gaussian blur the merged layer a little to create a more diffuse effect. I used a radius of 6 for the blur.

Now if we use a Screen blending mode on this layer, all the dark areas drop away and we are left with only nice blurry light areas on top of our original image.

3

This is a really useful way to use the Dodge blending modes: If you want to soften something up because you feel the lighting is too harsh, duplicating the original – bringing out the light areas – and then blurring and using a screen blending mode, gives us a much softer look.

Compare our end result to the original:

Lighting

The Lighting blending modes (**Overlay**, **Soft Light**, **Hard Light**, **Vivid Light**, **Linear Light**, and **Pin Light**) emphasize the white areas of an image, their role is in between dodging and burning, partially displaying or hiding different tonal ranges.

A good use for these would be if you want to paint some additional color onto your image, but still want it to blend in. Zooming in a bit, we draw (onto a new layer) a band of white using a size 13 soft edged brush:

A bit harsh, so let's add a Gaussian blur of 5:

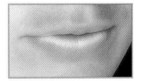

3

Notice that the white stands out a bit – it's a bit artificial, so to complete this task we're going to use the **Soft Light** blending mode. These blending modes allow the color and highlight to coat the image but let through the different tonal ranges – kind of like looking at the world through cellophane. So the pink of the lips is just made slightly lighter.

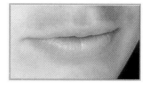

As you will notice, the color of the image is a bit off now. To fix this, we're going to paint over the affected areas using a skin colored hue then use the **Hue** blending mode.

So why use this blending mode? With the **Light** blending mode (such as in our lips example), the original color of the image still permeates through. This is great when you want to blend altered color with the original color in a natural way. What we're looking to do now however is largely change the original color. We've got a fairly nasty yellow and red tinge to the tonal range of the skin, brought on by our use of blending modes – unavoidable, but problematic.

We need to apply some virtual makeup to fix this. I used RGB value #F8A472 as my skin tone, changed the blending mode of the layer to hue, and then started painting over the affected areas.

I dropped the opacity of this layer to 35% so that we still had *some* of the original color coming through, albeit not much.

Compare the two images below. I've added a layer above everything else and filled it with 100% opacity pure red. The one on the left is using **Soft Light** – which gives everything a reddish tinge – but allows through the original colors. The one on the right is using **Hue**, which basically just makes everything red.

So we've fixed the skin texture and tone just using layers, but things are looking a little washed out. Let's add a bit of contrast. The skin still isn't perfect, so let's use a technique that will smooth the skin out even more:

I momentarily turned off the background layer, and then did another copy merged.

This merged layer doesn't take the background layer as part of it, so we're effectively just doing a merge of all our special effects. Notice that our new merged layer (called: *another merged*) is slightly transparent itself. This is because none of our layers are fully opaque. Our original '*merged*' layer (which is now acting as our bottom/background layer) is using a **Soft Light** blending mode – and because we have our background turned off, it is blending the **Soft Light** with transparency.

To this new merged layer, I applied a median filter (**Filter > Noise > Median**) with a radius of around 6. Usually this filter is used to reduce the effects of motion, but here we're using it to isolate and create areas of flat tone. Basically this filter blends the brightness of pixels within an area by creating an average and then applying this average to all pixels of similar tonal range.

Here, I've applied a Median filter using a radius of 22 (everything within a radius of 22 pixels will be forced into using the same tonal range):

As you can see, this filter gives the image a nice smooth watercolor look. Using this effect on our image, we smooth out the tone of the skin and also reintroduce a bit of contrast, thanks to our **Soft Light** blending mode.

Finally, to remove the stubborn blotches, simply create a new layer and use a soft edged brush of low opacity (15%) using your color picker to select a nearby skin tone and then paint over the affected areas. Here is the final result:

Use SHIFT + (plus sign) or SHIFT-(minus sign) to scroll through the Blending modes

Masking

If you're not familiar with masks, not to worry. Masks work pretty much the same way as grouping layers. Masks work by hiding areas of the layer without deleting them. When you draw on a mask, drawing in black is like erasing that part of the layer, and white means that part of the layer is properly displayed – for different levels of opacity grays are used.

So filling your mask layer with black means the layer is basically invisible, while filling it with white means the entire layer is visible. Often we will want to create a layer and then, using a black mask, hide the entire layer so that we can use white paint on the mask to paint bits of it in as we go.

3

Mask shortcuts

- SHIFT+ALT+click the icon at the bottom of the Layers palette, to create a mask layer that is automatically filled with black. Similarly, CTRL/CMD+ALT+click to create a mask filled with 50% gray.

- If you have a selection that you wish to make into a mask, you can do this by clicking on the **Add layer mask** button at the bottom of the Layers palette. A mask is then created filling the interior of our marquee with white, and everything else with black. The selection will be the only part of the layer showing.

- Alternatively, if you hold the ALT key as you press the **Add layer mask** button, then the mask is inverted; the selected part of the image will be made invisible.

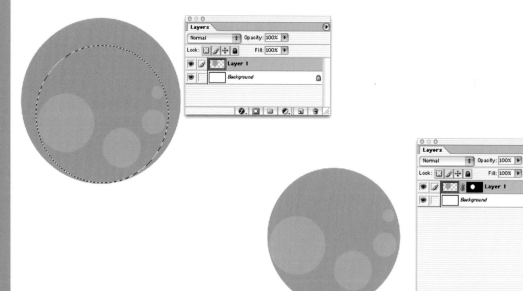

Manipulating masks

The great part about masks however is that they can be manipulated at any point. Ever delete part of an image only to find out later that you actually needed it?

If we'd used the Eraser tool to remove the outside part of the circle – as we did above, we'd be pretty stuck if we wanted to put it back. With masks, all we need to do is draw with white paint on the mask and the part of the image that was hidden is once again revealed:

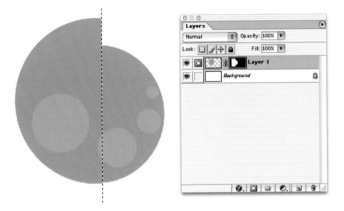

All we've done here is fill the left hand part of the mask with white, and as you can see, the part of the image that was hidden, is once again revealed.

Unlinking masks

Masks do not have to remain linked to their host image. As we'll see, it is possible to unlink them to create interesting results.

3

This means you can move the image around and leave the mask where it is. Here's an image that we can use in a mask:

Here's how the image looks masked: here's how it looks with the image moved:

Vector masks

Sometimes we need to make fairly complex masks. Let's say that we wanted a mask to look like this:

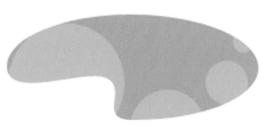

Now what happens if we want to change this shape? Currently our Layers palette looks something like this:

 The great part about using vector masks is that we can come back and easily modify them just like we'd modify any vector shape or work path.

What if we want to change this shape? Well we'd have to basically redraw the entire mask from scratch, which is a bit of a pain. Instead of drawing the selection, what we can do instead is CTRL click the new layer mask icon. This will give us a vector mask, instead of a layer mask. What this means, is that we can use vector shapes as our masks.

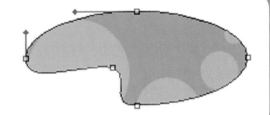

3

Removing Layer Masks

It's easy enough to remove a layer mask if you no longer need it – right/CTRL-click the mask thumbnail and select **Delete Vector Mask**. You can also temporarily disable a mask by right/CTRL-clicking and choosing **Disable Layer Mask**.

Alternatively you can SHIFT-click on the mask to toggle it on and off

Fill layers

When making color adjustments, it can be useful to add a color to a layer and then attach a mask to manipulate this color. The idea is that you then fill the mask with black and use white to paint over the mask. Then blending modes can be used to further emphasize the effect. In this example we have magically changed the color of the car.

Open your image, and create a layer above the layer you wish to manipulate.

Then add a fill layer **Layer > New Fill Layer > Solid Color**, which means we fill a layer with color and automatically attach a mask.

3

Now click on the mask and fill it with black. Then set your foreground color to white and carefully paint over the car to see the green color come through.

> You can also use a loaded selection in a Fill Layer for the mask, the selection can be loaded either before or after the mask is created.

Adjustment Layers

Adjustment Layers are a great way to color correct your images whilst maintaining a high degree of flexibility. They allow you to make all your adjustments on their own separate layer, so that if you change your mind later on, your original remains intact. Let's look at a way of using Adjustment Layers effectively.

1. Take an image, any image.

2. Click on the little black and white circle icon at the bottom of the Layers palette, this is the **Create new fill or adjustment layer** icon. Select **Hue/Saturation** from the ensuing pop up menu.

3. Adjust the Hue slider to your taste and press OK.

4. The Hue/Saturation now has its own layer in the Layers palette, and the image has changed accordingly.

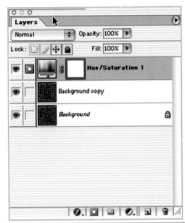

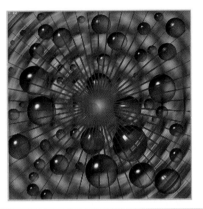

Merging Layers

Merging elements using Layer Masks

Here we have two pictures, which we want to smoothly blend them together. This effect is very pleasant to look at and seems very complex, but in fact, its very easy effect to achieve.

(For more detailed tutorials on blending, please see **Photoshop Most Wanted** also by friends of ED).

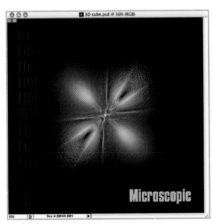

3

1. You can use any two images or download these two from our web site, www.friendsofed.com

2. Go to the Layers palette of the first image, click on the layer you want to move over, and simply drag it into the second image. This will create a new layer with the first image. To center it, hold down the SHIFT key while dragging.

3. If your two images are drastically different in size then you may need to use the Free Transform option to scale them to fit.

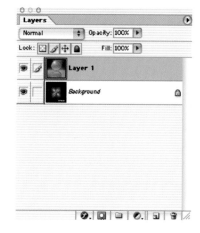

4. Press the **Add layer mask** icon at the bottom of the Layers palette.

You will see a Layer Mask attached to your image layer. When the Layer Mask is completely white, this is called **Reveal All** mode, and you can see your entire layer. To edit the mask you need to be able to see the little mask icon, if this is not visible, click on the mask thumbnail. When you paint over the Layer Mask in black then those areas mask the layer beneath, whereas white areas will reveal the layer, grayscale will produce different levels of transparency.

5. Choose the Gradient tool, (G), and select a linear, foreground to background gradient. Set the default colors by pressing the D key.

6. Drag the gradient from the top to the bottom of the image. Look in the Layers palette to see how this gradient has affected the Layer Mask.

7. Your final result will be similar to the one shown here. This effect will work for many different types of images and produce stunning collages with ease.

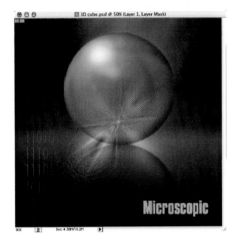

If you quickly want to merge two layers together, simply select the layer topmost in the palette, and click CTRL/CMD+E and the topmost layer merges down as per the **Layer > Merge Down** *menu command. This is an excellent timesaver for quick merging. SHIFT+CTRL/CMD+E allows you to merge all visible layers.*

Golden rules when merging layers

- If you are merging layers with styles or blending modes applied to them, there are certain things to remember. The bottom layer's mode will be dominant for styles, for example, if you have a layer with a bevel above a layer without and you then merge down, the two layers will flatten, losing the ability to edit the style.

- If the bottom layer contains a style, then the top layer will have its own styles flattened, and the bottom layer's styles will be applied and editable. Similarly for blending, the modes will flatten and multiply the effects with the bottom layers blending mode still active. You will learn more about blending layer mode later in this chapter.

- Have you ever tried to group a whole lot of layers using the **Merge Linked** command? If so, you will probably have noticed that the results are not quite what you expected. The reason for this is that when merging layers together, Photoshop treats all layers as if they have no blending modes. The only way to merge layers and preserve the blending mode is to link two together and merge them two at a time.

- Merging layers is tricky, because sometimes (usually much later!) you realize you shouldn't have done it! **Copy Merged** can be used as a lifesaving workaround in some situations – it allows you to test the effects of merging layers without the permanence of actually doing so. Go to **Edit > Copy Merged**, (Shift+Ctrl/Cmd+C). when you have an active selection on your canvas, and then this command will take a snapshot of everything that is visible within that selection, with the option of pasting this onto a new layer.

Layer sets

Managing the Layers palette with layer sets

Most of the time you end up merging layers because you've just got too many to handle. An alternative to merging is to use layer sets, which work a lot like folders. Layer sets offer a great way to organize your layers, and unlike merging, it is easy to edit individual objects within the group.

In this image, there are four folders; the folder named 'navigation' is currently open to reveal the layers inside it. There is also one layer, 'watermark', which is outside all the other folders.

You can create a layer sets simply by clicking on the folder icon at the bottom of the layers palette, or go **Layer > New > Layer Set**. Creating layer sets means that when you have the set selected, you can move all the layers it contains in one go, without needing to link them together.

*To put a bunch of layers into a new set all at once, link all the layers you want in the set and then use the Layer popup menu and choose **New Set From Linked**.*

When you create a layer set, you will notice that it has a special blending mode, **Pass Through**. This basically means that the layer set has no blending properties of its own. If you give the layer set a different blending mode then this will totally alter your whole image. First the layers in the layer set are composited, and then this new composite is treated as a single image, which is blended with the rest of the image using the selected blending mode.

Layer sets allow you to move a number of layers around in the layer hierarchy easily, even with Adjustment Layers and other grouped layers applied. Normally, if you move an Adjustment layer around in the hierarchy without its host layer, the grouping would be destroyed. By placing these symbiotic groups of layers into layer sets, we can safely move them around without this risk.

One last cool point for neatness freaks, putting layers in a set means that all you have to see is the layer set name – you don't waste your life scrolling through endless layers. It's also a convenient way to find the layer you want. If, by some not unreasonable chance, you have 60 layers in your design, you've got a much better chance of finding a specific layer if it has been assigned to an appropriately created set.

You can create a layer set, and add to it by dragging and dropping layers into it at any time. If you create a new layer when you have the layer set, or any layer within it selected, the new layer will be created within that layer set.

3

Using layer sets to store unwanted layers

Often we have layers that we no longer seem to need, but we don't want to risk the permanency of deleting them, just in case. Make a new layer set, name it Layer Trash (or whatever) and drag and drop the unwanted layers into there. This keeps them handy for later use, should they be needed, but more importantly keeps them out of the way. Keep this set just above the background, and keep it hidden. You can always delete the entire set, and take out the garbage, later. This is VERY handy for images with lots of layers.

Flexibility is a Photoshop buzz word, many people will advise you to build flexibility into your working practices – always be prepared to go back and change something, as you never know when a client, or you, will change their mind.

Creative combination of layers and their blending modes not only allow you to create amazing visual results, but also are the key to this freedom as they enable us to preserve the original image, which naturally makes it much easier to go back and make changes later.

4: Retouching

It's magic! Whether you're bringing new life to your own snapshots or making improvements on a client's photo, the art of retouching and correcting photos can make you feel like a wizard! Before digital photo manipulation came along, a photo that was too yellow, badly composed, or showed blemishes presented a real problem. Either we put up with it or we relied on special darkroom techniques, which not only required years of experience, but also the small matter of a darkroom itself!

Now, without getting our hands dirty or inhaling noxious fumes, we can do amazing things to repair, restore, retouch, and refresh our photos. This work is not easy, and no book can make it so. But in this chapter, we'll offer you some tips and techniques to guide you toward working magic on your own photos.

In this chapter, we will offer tips in the context of extended examples, illustrating the most common problems. Naturally each of your own photos will present its own unique challenges. Herein lies much of the fun and much of the hair pulling inherent in such work.

General retouching tips

Keep your original photo pristine

Always keep an unedited copy of your photo – this is the golden rule of retouching.

Before you even begin to work on a photo, save it as a PSD using a different filename, (so go to **File > Save As**). If you have layers in your document, check **Layers** in the dialog box to preserve these.

This leaves your original file pristine. No matter how good you are at fixing your photos now, you are not as good as you are going to be. Leave those originals intact so that you can return to them at a later date.

If possible, burn your photos onto a CD; this is safe, permanent storage that you can't accidentally erase.

Save your work as you go

- Save your work every few minutes as you go along. As you progress through your project, it is amazing how much work you can get done in an apparently small amount of time.

- When your power hiccups, and you know that it will, don't be caught asking yourself, "When was my last save?" If you have to ask, you will not want to know the answer. It is always "Too long ago".

- CTRL/CMD+S is easy, fast, and effective. Learn it. Love it. Live it. Whenever you achieve something you are happy with, no matter how small a detail it is, save it.

4

Plan ahead

By planning what you are going to do before you start working on a photo, you can save yourself a good deal of time. Opening your document and assessing what your problems are will give you the advantage of knowing your goals before you begin. It is most annoying to have spent an afternoon working on removing blemishes from the backdrop of a photo, only to decide later that you need to replace the background completely.

Before you start – essential preparation

Ideally, we'd all like to compose our photos as we shoot them, but if the photo is already taken, this is a luxury we don't have. You can still work affect the composition, however, through clever cropping of the photo.

Composition through cropping

You can completely change the focus, mood, and meaning of a photo, depending upon how you choose your cropping boundaries. Don't always center your subject. Cropping with your subject to one side can make your image seem more dynamic, or even unsettling or unpredictable, if that is your goal.

Here is one photo cropped in two very different ways: The first gives us a view of the old man in context, the second makes the mood more intimate by bringing us in closer to the subject.

Crop the photo first

Why? Cropping the photo will reduce its file size, reducing the load on your computer's resources. Photoshop is pretty demanding anyway. Don't waste its resources by asking it to make changes on image data that you are not going to need. Be sure you aren't going to need this data later however, as once you crop you can't get it back

*If file size is not an issue, then when cropping select **Hide** instead of **Delete** in the Options bar. By doing this, you can extend the cropped area beyond your canvas, and reclaim it later if necessary.*

Getting the big picture

4

If your photo takes up too much of your canvas, it is difficult to get a good idea how you want your cropping to look. If you want to see more of the picture while you are cropping, then zoom out. Here's how you can do it without losing the cropping boundaries you have already started:

1. Hold down ALT+SPACEBAR, and then click your image to zoom out. Use CTRL/CMD+SPACEBAR+click to zoom in.

2. When you release these keys, you'll still have your Crop tool and you can adjust your borders. This works if you want to zoom whilst using other tools too.

Duplicating your layer

Once you have cropped your image, duplicate your photo layer and lock it to prevent it being altered. That way you have a good visual reference to your original without having to open up your saved original file. You also have a ready backup should you accidentally do something to your photo that you cannot undo in the default 20 steps of the History palette.

You can actually set your History palette to record up to 1000 states, although whether or not this is practical depends on the memory you have available. To change it, go to **Edit > Preferences > General**.

4

Correcting tonal values

One of the first things to do when you are fixing a photo is to correct your tonal values and your colors. As with anything in Photoshop, there are at least three ways to accomplish these goals.

Levels and Curves

For lightening a photo, and improving contrast, both Levels and Curves are useful tools. Curves are more versatile than Levels, but also very touchy, so it's a good idea to reach for Levels first.

The Levels adjustment permits you to re-map your image's tonal values. That is, YOU determine that all the colors darker than a certain level are dead black and that all colors lighter than another level are dead white. You also determine the range of brightness your midtones will have.

Quick Levels adjustment

For a quick Levels adjustment, use the sliders under the histogram. Move the slider on the left, the black one, to the right, until only the tones that you want to be true black are black. This is often just inside where the histogram graph begins.

Then move your right, white slider toward the center, till it lines up with where the histogram begins from the right. Finally, move the middle slider till your photo looks good to you.

In this picture the bear is slightly too dark. We can use Levels to increase the contrast, to emphasize his face.

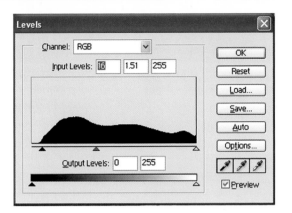

If you move either your black or white slider too close to the center, you will lose tonal information from your image. This is because, by moving the Levels sliders, you are redefining your true black, true white, and midtone. Any pixels represented in the histogram that lie to the left of the black slider become true black, losing any grayness or detail that they had. There are effects for which you want to convert grays to black, but in most photo work, you want to preserve as much image information as you can.

Make frequent use of Adjustment Layers

Adjustment Layers enable you to make changes to your image without touching your original pixels. It is as if you were putting a fancy overlay on your image – an overlay with which you can change or even eliminate the color. Adjustment Layers can also be used to selectively change the tonality, apply a gradient map, make a threshold adjustment, invert all of the colors, or to perform a number of other tasks!

The advantages of using Adjustment Layers

- They leave your original pixels intact and completely editable.

- They can be altered at any time. By double-clicking on the icon for the adjustment layer, there is your dialog box again, right where you left it, displaying your same settings, and completely editable.

- They come with their own built-in mask, too, so that you can apply this adjustment to any part of a layer, without it affecting the whole image.

- They can be grouped with an individual layer or a layer set, so that they only affect that layer or set, or left ungrouped so they affect all the layers below.

Spot Levels correction

The bear's eyes still seem to lack intensity.

To remedy this, we can do a spot Levels correction. Begin by making a selection of the areas that need the correction.

To add to a selection, once you have made it, hold the SHIFT key and select with any of the selection tools.

4

Once you get the eyes selected, click the **Create new adjustment layer** button at the bottom of the Layers palette. Choose Levels from the drop-down menu.

This brings up the Levels dialog box. Notice, too, that, in the Layers palette, the Adjustment Layer mask is black, all except for the selected area – the eyes. This means that your adjustments will just apply to the eyes.

By adjusting the sliders as shown here, we really bring this beautiful Kodiak bear to life!

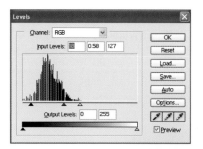

Correcting color

After the lightness/darkness is taken care of to your satisfaction, have a look at the color of your photo. This is the next thing to correct, before we go on to more specific problems.

Discerning color casts

There are several ways to analyze a photo's color. If you trust your own eyes, they will probably give you the best indication. If you want a more objective look, though, there are some other methods you can use.

The Info palette

One quick way to tell if your photo has an all-over off-color cast to it is to use the **Info** palette. Drag your cursor over the image, watching the RGB numbers. When your cursor is over an area that should be neutral, like white or gray, the RGB numbers should be very close to each other. If one is more than a few points higher than the others, you have a bit of a color cast.

 *By default, this palette is nested with your Navigator. If you can't see it, go to **Window > Info**, and it will come to the front.*

Using the Eyedropper

There is an easier way to get useful color information, especially if that Info palette gives you the heeby-jeebies:

1. Click the Foreground Color swatch at the bottom of the toolbar.

2. Bring the cursor over your image, and it will turn into an Eyedropper. Click on a part of the image where you are pretty sure what the color should be.

3. Now look at the color it actually is on your picker. If you think you have white, and it shows up as a very light value on the red palette, then you know you have to deal with a bit of a red cast.

In this example, even without looking at the image as a whole, but by looking at some samplings from the white shirt, we can see that there is a definite red cast to the image. A Color Balance adjustment fixes the color on her shirt, but it still doesn't fix all of the redness. Her complexion needs some special attention.

Localized color correction

What do you do when one small area of your photo needs an adjustment, but the rest of the photo is okay? Here's one way to deal with this. Use the handy little built-in mask that comes free with the Adjustment Layer!

1. First, make the Adjustment Layer (**Layer > New Adjustment Layer > Color Balance**) and, ignoring the rest of your photo, slide your sliders on the adjustment until the problem area looks good. Click OK.

2. Click the mask for your Adjustment Layer. Press D to restore the default colors, and ALT+BACKSPACE to fill the mask with black. This turns off the light on this layer, making your correction invisible.

3. Press X to switch your foreground and background colors. This gives you a white foreground.

4. Choose a soft brush and now paint on your image, in the area where you don't want the mask to hide your correction, to "turn the light back on" on that part of the layer. Cool, eh?

This method of spot correction allows you a good deal of control, is very versatile, and is completely reversible! Let's step through an example of it in action.

1. For the Casual Portrait, choose a Hue/Saturation adjustment layer to lose some of that red in her face. By picking the red channel in the drop-down, we are able to edit just the red.

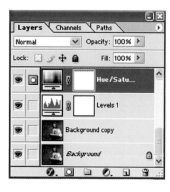 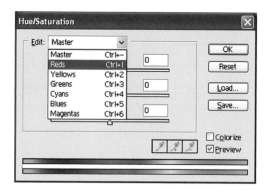

2. Pull the lightness slider up just a bit and choose OK. Her face looks appropriately toned at this point, but the reds in the rest of the image are too washed out. Let's use a mask to keep the color adjustment where we want it.

4

3. Click the mask for this Adjustment Layer. Fill the mask with black, making the correction disappear completely. Choose a soft white brush and then paint over her face.

4. Ok...we have fixed that over-red look, but now she looks almost pallid. How about adding some of that red back, in the form of lip tint and blush for her cheeks? Choose a small black brush and click that same mask. Paint it carefully over her lips and then choose a bigger soft brush for a light touch on her cheeks.

Here is a close up of what the painted mask looks like.

When retouching it is a good idea to zoom right in to pixel level, this avoids seeing the person in terms of eyes, mouth and nose, but simply as a collection of pixels. At this level you can see all the tiny variations of color that make up a person's face: You can deal with what is actually there, not with what you think should be there.

4

Making a micro view window

When you are working in micro view, zoomed in on your subject, it is important to keep one eye on what you are doing to your big picture. A good way to do this is to create a micro view window.

1. With your file open, click on **Window > Documents > New Window**. This will bring up another working copy of your document.

2. Choose your Zoom tool and check **Resize Windows To Fit** in the Options bar.

3. Hold the ALT key and zoom out, making your picture very small, as small as you want your micro view window to be.

4. Now uncheck Resize Windows, and using your Zoom tool, drag out a rectangle around the area you want in micro view.

5. Click your Zoom tool on your picture until you are as close as you want to be.

When you make changes to one view, the changes will occur in the other window as you make them!

Digital make-overs

Whitening teeth

Even the whitest teeth can be improved by a bit of whitening. While you are doing this, though, remember that you don't want to over-whiten, or you will end up with a phony look. Keep in mind, too, that the teeth in the front will look considerably whiter than those behind.

If RAM is an issue for you, when you make a correction to just part of your picture, you can do this on a mini-layer! Select just that part, in this case, the mouth area, and use Ctrl/Cmd+J *to copy it to a new layer. Be sure to label this layer. It gets confusing to have unlabeled body parts in the layers palette!*

4

There are several ways to whiten teeth. One way is to use the **Dodge** tool. It looks like a black magnifier and is next to the Blur tool in the toolbox. Before you start this, it is a good idea to copy the layer on which you will be working.

The Dodge tool lightens the tones of the area without losing the color (unless you get too light.) It is a cumulative effect, so that the more you rub it over the area, the lighter it gets. Using a setting of 25% exposure will make your effect more gradual and easy to control. For these teeth, I had the best success using the Midtones range and a feathered brush about the width of the smallest tooth. The exact size will vary depending upon the size and resolution of your project image.

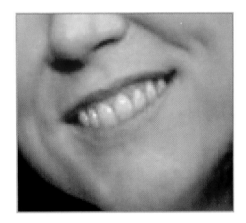

Another way of doing this would be to create a new layer, and while creating it, set the blending mode to soft light. Now if we paint on this new layer, with a soft-edged fairly low opacity (10%) brush we can gradually whiten the teeth, without affecting the original layer.

A digital face lift

Now let's remove some of the years etched on her face. Draw a loose selection around her face with the Lasso tool and press Ctrl/Cmd+J to copy her face to a new layer before you begin this. This creates a new face lift layer, so that if you make a mistake, you are not messing up your actual image.

Next, go over your image and get an idea for the areas that you want to fix.

4

How to heal without scars

The **Healing Brush** tool uses a color-averaging algorithm to reproduce the existing texture with the colors from the source you designate. Or to put it another way - the Healing Brush tool can work miracles and is very cool!

If you try to use the Healing Brush in an area of high contrast, you can get infection from the neighboring colors. To avoid this, use a selection around the target area you are healing. You can still use a source outside of this selection.

Since you can't heal onto a separate layer, as you can with the Clone tool, always duplicate the working layer before you begin this process. This will protect your image in case you make a mistake which history cannot undo.

1. If you are working with an area that has contrasting colors close to it, begin by making an unfeathered selection around it. (Feathering the selection will make the contrasting area encroach upon your healing.)

2. Choose your Healing tool, and select an appropriately sized brush tip for it.

3. Hold the ALT key and your cursor will turn to the crosshairs in a circle, you can see this on the left of our image below. This is to sample the area where Photoshop will get the texture/color to graft into your problem area, your 'wound'.

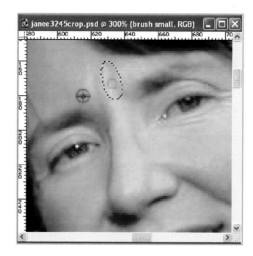

4. Release the ALT key and move your cursor over to the wound.

5. As you paint over the wound, it will look just as if you are cloning. That is, until you lift your brush! That is when Photoshop goes to work with its pixel-averaging!

 Repeatedly stroking the region you are healing will often improve it, but if it doesn't, you may do better with either a different source, or with a different method of retouching.

Patching things up

The **Patch** tool is pretty cool, too. It works a bit like the Healing Brush tool, in that it uses a similar algorithm to blend the patch into the existing selection.

The Patch tool is handy to use for larger areas that are relatively homogeneous, that is, there is not much detail. The Patch tool does not work well when its boundary, for either the source or the destination) is close to another contrasting color. This is because Photoshop averages the Patch pixels in with what is surrounding. If there are contrasting colors or tones very close, you will end up with the contrasting tone bleeding into your patched area.

1. First, be sure that you have the right layer, your working layer, chosen in the Layers palette, and select the Patch tool from under the Healing Brush in the toolbox.

2. Next, you have to identify your destination area, in other words the area that needs correction. So, in the Options bar check the **Destination** radio button.

3. Now use the Patch tool to draw a selection around the part you want to replace.

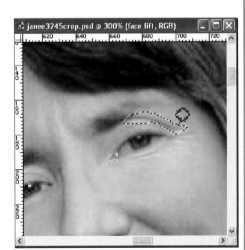

4. Now to identify your source area, this is the region from which you make your patch. Choose the **Source** radio button in the Options bar. Bring your Patch tool inside the selection and it will turn into the Patch Mover.

5. Drag this patch outline to where you want Photoshop to get your patch... Release your mouse and you've patched!

> *In our attempts to retouch, we are often so dazzled by the new tools available to us that we can forget the simple ways to correct little flaws. For the little place on her left jaw and her chin, Photoshop's Dodge tool works beautifully. Be sure to do this work in your Micro View window. Then check your work in your main window.*

4

Blur painting

This is another old stand-by, and there are some problems with it, but it still has its uses.

1. Duplicate your working layer. In the example, the face layer upon which we have been doing the healing, patching, and dodging is the working layer.

2. Select the bottom of these two duplicate layers in the Layers palette and label it Blur.

3. Turn off the eye on your working layer so that you can see your Blur layer.

4. Go to **Filter > Blur > Gaussian Blur**. The amount of blur you use will depend upon the resolution of your photo and upon the size of the flaws you are trying to get rid of. In general, your blur should be enough that the features are not readily recognizable, and your flaw should not be visible.

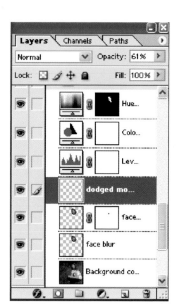

5. Turn your working layer's eye back on and then click that layer in the Layers palette to make it active.

6. Click the Add Layer Mask icon at the bottom of the Layers palette.

7. Choose a soft brush that is about the same thickness as your flaw, or maybe a bit larger. In your Brush Options, be sure that your brush dynamics are turned off for this.

8. Type D to set the Default colors, and then reduce the opacity of your brush to 30% or so and then paint away your blemishes!

What's going on here? You are actually painting black/gray on the layer mask, which "turns the light off" in the working layer, letting the Blur layer show. Note that you are not really altering the working layer by doing this! By painting white back on the mask, you can undo this!

For this example, we can use blur painting to soften that exaggerated smile line under her mouth on her right side.

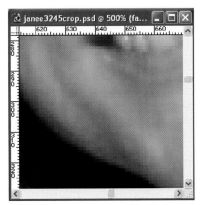 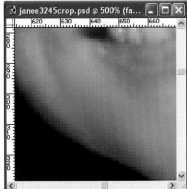

> This technique is useful, but it is not the perfect answer for everything, because you tend to lose texture, so use it carefully!

The Clone Stamp tool

Before we get to grips with using this tool let's explore the two cloning options available to us – the **Working Layer Clone** or the **Use All Layers Clone**. If your image has an Adjustment Layer, you need to use the Working Layer Clone.

Working Layer clone

1. Select the Clone tool by clicking S.

2. Duplicate the layer from which you are getting your clone. This new copy will be your cloning working layer.

3. Then uncheck **Use All Layers** in the Clone tool Options bar. You will still see the image and the cloning through the Adjustment Layers, but your cloning will actually be occurring on the unadjusted layer, using this layer for the sampling source.

In Working Layer Cloning, you don't have the freedom to manipulate your cloning layer separately, and it can be difficult to make little changes in your work.

Use All Layers clone

This is my preferred way to clone most of the time, because all of the cloning goes to its own clean layer. When you clone onto a separate layer, you can manipulate this cloning layer just as you can manipulate any separate layer: blurring, using filters, layer effects, masking, using layer blending modes, as well as having the convenience of easy correcting. Here's how to do Use All Layers cloning:

- Make a new layer above all the rest

- Check **Use All Layers**

- ALT-click your source area, and paint onto your destination

This method uses all of the layers that are visible and clones that information onto the new layer. It will seem to you that you are working just on the new layer, while your clone-sample is being taken from all the layers.

4

Cloning when you have Adjustment Layers

Working Layer Cloning is depicted here in A. If you are using Adjustment Layers, as we do in this example, you will probably want to use this method. Use All Layers Cloning is depicted in B. This method uses any visible layers to clone onto the new layer.

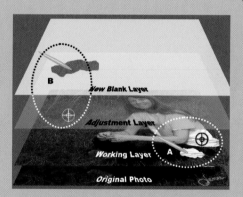

When you clone onto a separate layer, you can manipulate this cloning layer just as you can any separate layer, by blurring, using filters, layer effects, masking, layer blending modes, as well as having the convenience of easy correcting.

In the diagram at B, you can see what happens when you do Use All Layers cloning on a separate layer above an adjustment layer. If you then make a change on the Adjustment Layer, the cloning layer will remain as it was, which could present a problem.

So why not just clone onto a new layer between the Adjustment Layers and your working layer? Well, to clone onto a blank layer, you have to do a Use All Layers clone. When you clone onto a clean layer, you have to clone from something. If you don't have Use All Layers checked in the Clone options, you are trying to clone from the blank layer onto the blank layer. This will lead to your wondering why the Clone tool is not working.

Using All Layers means that it will clone from everything that is visible, both above and below your layer, including the Adjustment Layers. This seems fine, except that, if you are cloning the adjusted colors onto a layer that is below the Adjustment Layers, the adjustment will occur twice to this cloning layer!

Ok, so let's clone her left eyebrow in that area where it is a bit thin. Since we have adjustment Layers, the Working Layer clone is the best approach. Duplicate the working layer and clone directly onto it.

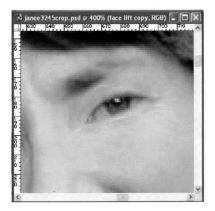 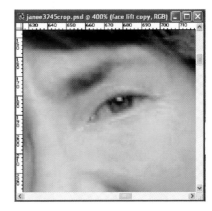

Here's our final image, we've digitally applied some make up to our subject too - the key word to all of this is subtlety. We don't see a huge difference from our original shot, but the effect is pleasingly professional.

Before   After

Red eye removal

There is a common problem with a lot of flash photography, which I'm sure you are all too familiar with, called red eye. This is when the flash causes the iris of the eye to expand suddenly, and if the flash is too close to the lens, it produces this devastating effect. This usually happens with flash photos taken in dark rooms when the flash is too close to the camera lens. Having supplemental lighting, having the subject not looking right into the camera, or using a preflash, present on some cameras, will help alleviate this.

We'll look at a couple of ways of reducing this effect, the first is a more traditional method, the second makes clever use of the Threshold command.

4

The traditional way

Zoom in nice and close so you can see what you are doing when you are working.

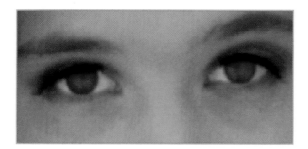

1. Choose the **Sponge** tool in the toolbar. In the top toolbar the Sponge tool options will be visible. Choose Desaturate, and a soft, smaller brush size – here I have used 13.

   When in Desaturate mode, the Sponge tool will remove all the color from the area you apply it. It will not, however, affect the tonal quality of the image.

2. Carefully paint over the redness of the eyes.

3. Now we want to add a bit of color back into the iris.

   Create a new layer and set the blending mode to **Color**.

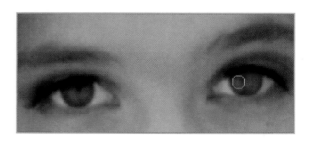

4. Choose a color for the eye. A little color goes a long way so make it a very pale color. Here we will make our eyes blue, using the following values: R 114; G 156; B 184.

5. Paint onto the eyes on the new layer. Notice how much color is applied to the image.

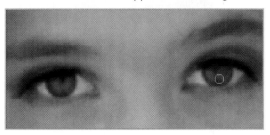

We need to make the color a bit more realistic.

6. Reduce the opacity of the color layer until you get a satisfactory result.

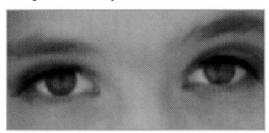

There! Much better.

7. Zoom back to see the entire image. It looks pretty good, but something is missing. The pupils need a bit of a boost.

8. Choose the Brush tool and press D to restore the default colors. Choose a small soft brush. In the tool options, set the opacity to 20%.

9. Create a new layer and name it pupil.

10. Just dab the brush once where the pupil is, to boost it a bit. If the brush is too big or too small, undo, (CTRL/CMD+Z) change the brush size and try again. This is an effect you will want to apply with just one dab, so it doesn't look like the person has 2 pupils.

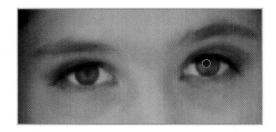

There you go. You'd never know your photo had suffered from red eye in the first place.

Using the Threshold command

It's not just people who suffer from redeye. In this photo of our canine friend, we see the retinal reflection presenting itself as a ghostly green.

Remember that not every method of red eye removal will yield satisfactory results in every situation.

The example above relies upon re-coloring the subject's eyes, and redoing the catch light (the little tiny white dot of reflected light in our subject's eyes). Such fine details can make or break the photo, so let's look at a method which allows us to change as little as possible, but still get rid of the offending reflection.

The next method works very well if your subject's iris is intact and the reflection is just apparent in the pupil. Since the only colors that should be present in the pupil are black, for the pupil, and white, for the catchlight, this method changes all the colors in the pupil area to either black or white. Here's how to do it:

1. Make a selection of the pupil areas. You can do them both together, holding SHIFT to add to the selection, or you can just do one first.

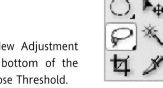

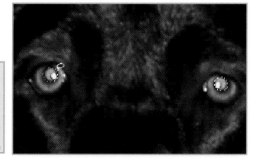

2. Click the Create New Adjustment Layer icon at the bottom of the Layers palette. Choose Threshold.

3. Move the slider on the Threshold adjustment over toward the left till all you have left is black and white, and your result looks pleasing. Click OK.

4

4. If you just did one eye, you can add the second eye in on this same layer.

5. Click the mask for the Adjustment layer in the Layers palette. It is the mostly black square on the right side.

6. Choose a hard round paintbrush and white, and paint over the second eye's pupil.

Restoring old photos

Cropping your problems away

Here I have a charming picture called Summer Cottage. It's far from perfect though; age has chewed the corners away. Also, there are parts around the edges where the photo is too light. The house next door, and the writing on the photo act as a distraction from the main image. Fortunately, as many of these problems are around the outside of the photo, we can crop away much of our work. Remember, though, to **always keep a copy of the original image.**

Coping with color in old monotone photos

It is a very rare monotone photo that scans in as a true monotone. Old photos will carry artifacts of age, uneven fading of tones, yellowing, or greening, In this micro view of Summer Cottage, many colors become evident – yellows, greens, and even pink.

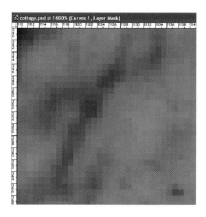

Since we are going for a monotone photo, these are not tones that we want in our finished image. Our first step, then, is to take out the color in these photos. Then, after we do the necessary cleanup, we will add back the color that we want.

4

Desaturating a photo

As with anything in Photoshop, there is a multitude of ways to remove color from, or desaturate, a photo. Here are four:

- **Image > Adjust > Desaturate**. This is the quickest way, but often the sloppiest, leaving behind artifacts, dust, and poor contrast.

- Add a Hue/Saturation Adjustment Layer and move the Saturation slider to the far left. This has the same effect as desaturate, but is reversible and adjustable, since it is on an Adjustment Layer.

- **Image > Mode > Grayscale**. This wholesale change will throw away any color information you have, including that which is in any layer of the image.

- **Channel Splitting**. This is more difficult to do, but can sometimes yield better results. This is the method used in our Summer Cottage example, here's how to do it:

    1. Save your PSD. Then go to **File > Save As...** and rename the file.

    2. Flatten any layers.

    3. Click on Split Channels in the drop-down on the Channels palette.

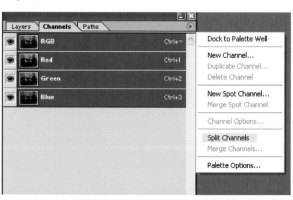

4. When you get the three files, choose the one that is cleanest and has the best contrast. For this example, the R channel yields the best contrast, though, with the B channel, the writing on the photo becomes much less apparent. This is where art meets science. You must simply choose the one with which you want to work.

Dealing with an unevenly faded photo

Working with adjustment layers only goes so far, when your photo is unevenly faded. At some point, you are going to have to do some manual work to fix this. Don't panic! You can learn to do this, even if you "can't draw".

Once we have lightened the Summer Cottage using levels and curves, we see that the edges are lighter than the central part of the photo. One tool with which we can even up the tones is the Burn tool.

After initial curves and levels adjustments, the edges are too light

We can fix this in the following way:

1. Duplicate your working layer by dragging the layer to the New Layer icon at the bottom of the layers palette, or press CTRL/CMD+SHIFT+N to create a New Layer..

2. Choose the Burn tool and set its exposure low, say 25%. This allows you to do the correction gradually.

3. Choose a broad soft airbrush tip, for a nice easy-does-it approach. You want your brush to be broader than the area in which you are working.

4. Use Create a New Snapshot if you are about to start something new. Then if your results are not as expected, you can revert to the image as it was at the time of the snapshot.

When you go too far

If you do overdo things while using the toning tools, painting, or cloning, you have several recourses.

- CTRL/CMD+Z to undo.

- CTRL/CMD+ALT+Z to undo multiple steps.

- Click up in your history palette to before the error.

- If you have goofed up more than your history palette will hold, you can lighten a burned area back a bit using a similar light touch with the Dodge tool, or use an Adjustment Layer to fix things.

- You can erase painting or cloning errors if they are on another layer.

- If you mess up to such a degree that you just can't fix it at all, then delete your layer (if you duplicated it!) and start again with another duplicate of your working layer.

4

Using Adjustment Layers to fix uneven fading

For the Summer Cottage, here is an alternative to the burn method used above. I used two Levels Adjustment Layers for this – one for the overall edge darkening, and then another to fine-tune it, darkening some areas further.

Here's how this works:

1. Create a new Levels Adjustment Layer, and move the sliders so that the darkest part is as light as you want it to be ultimately. The rest of the image will get way too light, but don't worry about that.

2. Choose black in the Foreground Color Picker and choose the Brush tool.

3. Click on the white mask for this Levels layer in the Layers palette and paint over any part of the image that is too dark. In this example there was much of it that had become too dark. If such is the case, it's a good idea to fill the mask with black and then paint the correction in with white.

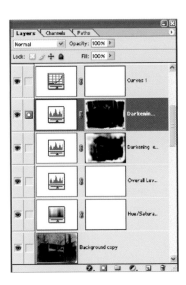 

4. If there are some other areas that are still too dark, you can add another Levels Adjustment Layer and repeat the process.

5. Drawing on the mask still requires some hand work, but it does have its advantages in that we can come back at any point and make changes, if we don't like the way things have turned out.

Fixing blemishes

Once we get the contrast and brightness fixed here, we can begin to tackle the flaws. The cracks, dust specks, and water fade marks are numerous, but with a micro-view and the Healing Brush tool, we can get rid of most of this damage. Remember these when using the Healing Brush tool:

- Duplicate your working layer first.

- Keep in mind the rule about healing near a contrasting area: use a selection.

- Be patient.

- And finally, remember to CTRL/CMD+S whenever you're happy with the effect.

Sharpen your photo last

Only sharpen after you are done with all your other corrections. The reason for this is that sharpening will only intensify some of the flaws you have. Also, sharpening changes the detail that is in your photo. Where there is contrast, Photoshop makes it firmer, creating a "sharper" edge. If you sharpen and then do other corrections, you will want to sharpen those corrections to go with the rest of your photo. Before long, you have a muddy mess.

Sharpening with the Unsharp mask

As with anything else in Photoshop, there are several ways to sharpen. It is important to first consider your goals with sharpening. For example, in the "Casual Portrait" above, you do not want to sharpen the whole photo, after you painstakingly softened all of those age tracks!

After adjusting the contrast for the Summer Cottage, it is apparent that this photo does need some sharpening. I would like to sharpen mainly the architectural details of the cottage, though, and not necessarily the background trees or the foreground landscaping.

Unsharp mask sounds like it will unsharpen your photo, but it actually does a pretty good job of sharpening. Duplicate your layer before you use this filter. Go to **Filter > Sharpen > Unsharp Mask**. This filter defines an edge, and then it increases the contrast between pixels on either side of this edge. You determine the edges; the amount of contrast, and how many pixels will be affected using the settings in the dialog box:

- **Amount** – decides how much contrast you want between the edge and surrounding pixels.

- **Radius** – the number of pixels from the edge where contrast will be increased.

- **Threshold** – defines the sensitivity of the "edge" determination. Higher numbers mean that pixels have to be very different in color in order for their boundary to be defined as an edge.

If you try to over sharpen, you will end up with an unpleasant "halo" effect.

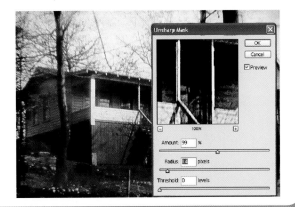

4

Sharpening with the High Pass filter

This filter is not one that I use every day. However, it can be used here to help define our edges to make a well-sharpened photo. What it does is to retain only edge pixels within the radius you assign. At the same time, it turns all non-edge pixels into a neutral gray. You will see more what it does by seeing the results for yourself:

1. Duplicate your working layer.

2. With the top working layer active, choose **Filter > Other > High Pass**.

3. Move the Radius slider toward the left, until only your edges are showing.

4. In the Layers palette, change the blending mode of this layer to Overlay.

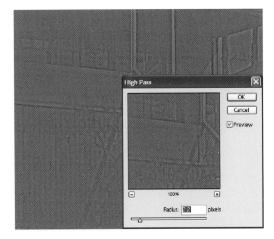

Here we see our image before the High Pass Filter was applied.

This picture shows the same area after the filter was applied.

Sharpening in Lab Color mode

To those of us who don't switch modes often, this might seem intimidating, but it is much less scary than it sounds, and you can end up with some nice results using this method of sharpening. Because this sharpening involves flattening any layers, it is especially important that you do this AFTER all other work.

For Lab Color sharpening, you will change your photo from RGB mode into **Lab Color** mode. This is a different way for Photoshop to define your colors, as evidenced in your **Channels** palette. Instead of controlling how much red, green, and blue light get to the canvas, you are controlling whether one light (a) is more red or green, and whether the second light (b) is more blue or yellow. The L is like a rheostat, which determines if the overall light is brighter or darker.

Before you switch to Lab Color mode, you have to flatten your layers, so it is very important that you do the first steps, as delineated here. When you sharpen in Lab mode, usually you will sharpen the L (lightness or luminance) channel. Here's how to proceed:

1. When you have done all other work to your photo, save your PSD once again, with its layers intact.

2. **File > Save as** and rename your file.

3. Flatten the layers in this new file.

4. **Image > Mode > Lab Color.**

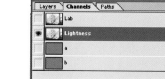

5. Click on the Channels tab and choose the Lightness channel.

6. **Filter > Sharpen > Unsharp Mask**.

7. Adjust your settings until you get a level of crispness you like.

8. Click on the Lab channel at the top of the layers palette, to get back your composite view.

9. **Image > Mode > RGB** to return it to RGB mode.

Combining sharpening methods

If you are not getting satisfactory results with any one sharpening method, you can combine methods, often with pleasing results. For example, since you saved the Lab mode sharpening separately above, you can use this as a layer in your original document and blend its results in, using a layer blending mode:

1. With both files open and your Lab-sharpened document active, type V for the Move tool.

2. Hold the Shift key and drag your Lab-sharpened layer over to your original document. (Holding Shift while you drag centers your layer in your new document.)

3. Change the layer blending mode of the Lab-sharp layer. Experiment with the blending modes, because you can get very different effects with each.

Selective sharpening

You can also use layer masks on sharpened layers to lower their intensity or to isolate their effect. For example, in this photo, I wanted more sharpening on the house than on the trees, so here's how I proceeded:

1. Duplicate the main working layer.

2. Use Unsharp mask on the topmost of these.

3. Click the Add layer mask button in the layers palette.

4. Using a large soft black airbrush (no dynamics), on the mask, paint away the parts that are over sharpened.

Adding the final touches by hand

This cottage photo had some really serious sharpening problems. One was the jittery roofline effect, which became only somewhat better through sharpening. The background trees still make me feel astigmatic, but I deem them ok.

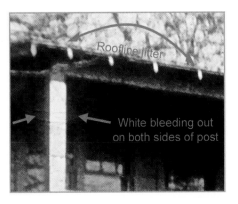

In doing all of this sharpening, we exaggerated the softness of the texture that was in some areas of the photo. We also played up the glaring lack of texture in some areas. This left us with speckled or mottled areas, which look ok from a distance, but really don't look good up close. How do we fix this?

We are back to that "texture" question. We really are in a position where we have to put in texture where there wasn't much to start with.

From where I sit, we have one good path left to follow, and this is to do some final hand-painting touchups.

Sample painting

When you are painting on a photo, you have a huge advantage from the start. Your colors are all given to you! When you are sample painting, heed the following:

- Paint on a separate layer. If you have adjustment layers, you will either need to turn them off as you paint, or you will need to paint on a layer above all of them. This will mean that if you make a change to an adjustment layer, it will not affect this painted layer.

- Keep one finger on your ALT/OPT key. When you are painting, to grab a color from your canvas, hold this key down. This transforms your brush to the Eyedropper temporarily, while you click your canvas and get the color.

- Be sure that your Eyedropper tool has the Point Sample option checked.

- As mentioned before, create a Micro View Window to use.

- Sample often, to pick up different shades, and use small strokes, especially if you are creating texture.

- CTRL/CMD+S to save... frequently.
- If the effect of your painting is too strong, use a lower opacity, blur the layer a bit, or try a layer blending mode.

- Another way to speed things, when creating a texture by hand painting, is to select an area and then use **Filter > Noise > Add Noise**.

In these pictures, I've shown the area to be corrected with red arrows. The hand-painted correction is in the other square box.

```
      BUILDING #19 1/6
         219 Lincoln Ave.
         Haverhill, MA
          978-373-1990


REGULAR            3428 1 00002 60430
SALE         0006 03/22/06  11:29 AM

  33 BOOKS  1 @ 14.98          14.98
 MA 5%   TAX                    0.75
     TOTAL                    $15.73
                 CASH          20.03
                 CHANGE         4.30


******************************************
     This is a RECEIPT ONLY!          *
******************************************
       EVERYTHING SOLD WITH OUR        *
       30 DAY *NO HARD TIME*           *
 MONEY BACK GUARANTEE WITH SALE SLIP   *
******************************************


          HAVE A CHEAP DAY
```

BUILDING #19 1/4

219 Lincoln Ave.
978-373-1990

****

            HAVE A CHEAP DAY

4

And here is the result at this point:

Putting color back into the photo

When we first began this project, we desaturated the monochrome, making it black and white. This helped us with the little color artifacts. Now that the photo is looking good, we want to add some color back. We won't try to replace that dreadful green/brown of the original, but instead, give it what we imagine it might have looked like before it faded. In this case, I opted for a warm sepia-like hue. Here's how to give your photo an all-over color tone:

1. Create a new Hue/Saturation Adjustment Layer.

2. Tick the Colorize box.

3. Move the sliders till you like the look and click OK.

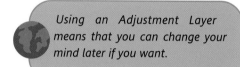

Using an Adjustment Layer means that you can change your mind later if you want.

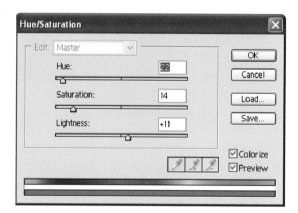

Create your own Color Cast

Yes, I know that Photoshop ships with a Sepia-Toning action. But I also know that if everyone used this action, all of our sepia photos would have the same hue. Were all sepias the same? No. They all were different, depending upon the processor, the chemicals used, and even upon the whim of the developer! Why should all modern-day sepia be the same? Go a little wild and create your own sepia!

Finishing the photo

Ultimately, I opted to crop a little closer, losing most of the neighbor's house. I added the photo border frame and here is the final result:

4

A restoration? That is a matter for debate. But I think that we can agree, that we have improved the photo significantly! This was not an easy job, to be sure, but the result was well worth it, both to me, and to my client!

Photoshop 7 provides us with some powerful retouching and correction tools, the Healing Brush and the Patch tools can work miracles with our pictures, but the real key to successful retouching and restoration is subtlety and patience. Gently does it should be your mantra. Also, in your rush to embrace the new tools, don't neglect the simple effectiveness of old favorites such as the Clone Stamp tool, sometimes the old ways really are the best

5: Special Effects

Photoshop is so much more than just a tool for manipulating photos. Photoshop can be used to make artwork from scratch, too. In this chapter, we will work with several different effects you can use to enhance your artwork. These include some very realistic text effects, ideas for site interface designs, and other useful things to help you make your work stand out.

We'll cover a variety of different kinds of effect,and show you the tools that you will need to customize them for your own use, and to create effects of your own. These include using filters, transformations, channels, and layer masks.

Zoom trail

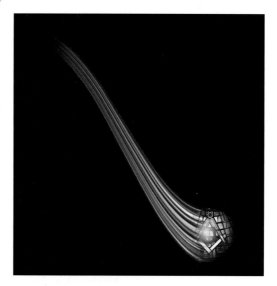

I really like this zoom trail effect. It is a much different effect from that of a motion blur, as you will see. It is also versatile, in that you can curve the trail and fade it. This is done using the powers of the Move tool, opacity, and masking.

For this example, I used a photo of a beautiful stained glass window, which I took at the National Heritage Museum in Lexington, Massachusetts, USA (http://www.monh.org).

Sampling the image for the zoom trail

There are many ways to do this, depending upon how you want your end effect to look. I opted to sample straight down the middle of the image for this. The colors along the edge of the selection are the ones that will appear in the zoom trail. The rest of the selection is actually superfluous, but I kept it here so that it would be easier to see what is going on. Which edge? It depends upon which direction you go with your trail. The colors along the trailing edge will show in the end. (This will make more sense in a minute.)

1. Select the part of your image containing the colors you wish to have in your zoom trail. Be sure, too, that the trail colors are along one **edge** of your selection.

2. CTRL/CMD+J to copy this selection to a new layer. This will be your Trail layer.

Making the zoom trail

1. Type V to choose the Move tool. With the Trail layer active in the layers palette, CTRL/CMD-click the trail layer to load it as a selection

2. Hold ALT with your left hand and use your right hand to operate the arrow key that is on the opposite side from your trail colors. (In this example, I used the left arrow, because the colors I want for my trail are on the right, where the selection cuts down the middle of my disk). If you just hold these keys down, your selection will replicate itself all the way across your screen.

3. Holding ALT with the Move tool will duplicate with each click. Clicking the arrow key is the same as a click of your mouse for this except that it gives you one-pixel movements.

4. Making the selection before copying it puts all of the copies onto ONE layer. Without selecting first, you quickly get many, many layers!

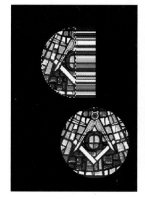 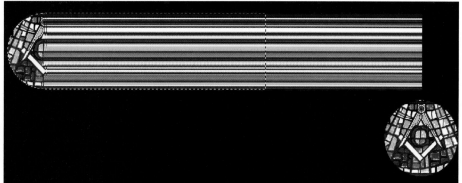

If your selection is large, or your RAM small, this might go slowly. If this happens, you can make a short string of replications and then stop. Ctrl-click the trail layer again, and then Ctrl-Alt-Shift and drag the copy over to the end of where it was. (Shift keeps your drag to 45 degree intervals, making it easier to keep your line straight.)

5. You can use this trail as it is, if you like, or you could put some curve in the zoom trail, and make it fade off into the distance.

6. To curve the trail, go to **Edit > Transform > Rotate**, then rotate it 90 degrees so that it is vertical.

7. If you are going to taper it, now is the time to do that as well. Hold CTRL/CMD while you have Free Transform open, this changes the command to the Distort command, then pull the bottom corners in until you have as much of a point as you want.

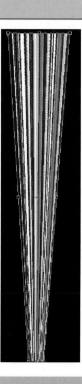

8. **Filter > Distort > Shear**. Watch the preview window and drag the curve till it is as you like it. The fewer points you add, the smoother your curve will be. If you find you have an unwanted point on the curve, click it and drag it off!

9. **Edit > Transform > Rotate** 90 degrees the other way.

10. Line the curve up with your disk. You may have to do some fine tuning and distorting to get it to fit. The curved trail will fit more easily onto the disk if you position the disk on a relatively flat area of the curve.

5

Making any disk into a planet

1. CTRL/CMD-click the disk layer to load it as a selection.

2. Add a new layer above the disk.

3. Drag a white to black radial gradient onto the new layer, across the selection, following the path of this arrow:

4. To constrain it, we need to have created a marquee around this area or the entire area will flood fill!

> *Another way to do this, would be to duplicate our Stained glass layer (which is the correct size and shape), lock the transparency of the layer, and then just fill away.*

5. Then change the blending mode of this layer to Luminosity.

6. Link the disk layer and the gradient layer and CTRL/CMD+E to merge them. This is optional, but makes it easier to deal with the planet as a unit.

7. If your trail extends beyond the planet, select the area you want hidden. Then hold ALT as you click the Add Layer Mask icon at the bottom of the layers palette. (Holding ALT makes the mask cover the selected area. When you don't hold ALT, the mask exposes only the selection.)

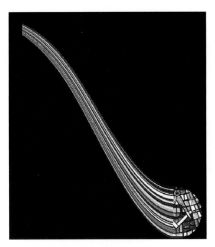 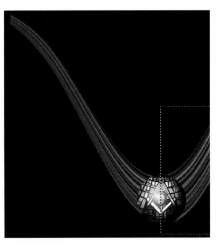

Now you need to reduce the opacity of the zoom trail layer, but probably not evenly. If you have a chopped tail end, as I do, you may want to fade that out, as well. You also want the trail to appear to encase the planet, as if the planet is creating the trail in its wake.

Here is the trail reduced in opacity to 50%.

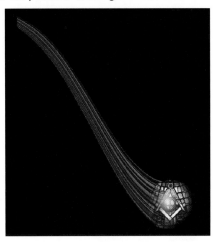

8. Here is one way to make the ball seem encased in the trail. Put the planet above the trail in the Layers palette. (If you did not merge the shading onto the disk, your planet will be in two layers.)

9. With the top planet layer clicked, CTRL/CMD+E to merge this down onto the other. (This is optional, and I did not merge. If you do not merge, you have to make a mask for each of the planet layers.)

10. Add a layer mask to the planet layer(s).

11. Click the planet layer mask and drag a black to transparent gradient from left to right, just across the diameter of the planet. This mask hides the left side of the planet, allowing the trail to look as if it is in the foreground.

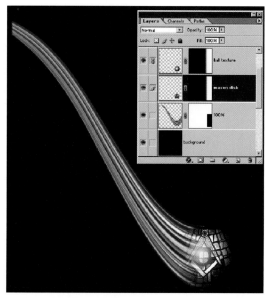

12. Now, reduce the opacity of the trail layer to about 50%.

13. Make the left side of the trail fade off by painting another black to transparent gradient on its mask.

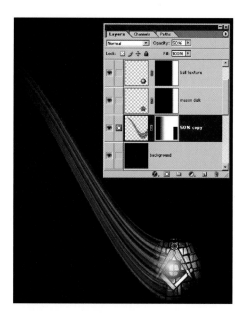

14. I wanted the right side of the trail to be less opaque, so I duplicated the trail layer - which is at 50% opacity, and added more to the black to transparent gradient on this layer's mask to give just the right amount of fade.

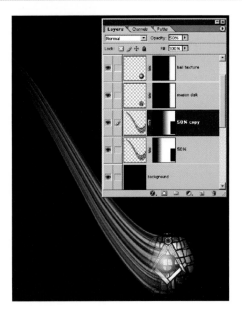

5

A final touch. I didn't like the zipper effect that came from the extreme bending with the Shear filter. I fixed this by adding just a wee bit of Gaussian blur to the top trail layer.

15. To bring back the nice sharp edge along the sides, CTRL/CMD+click the bottom trail in the layers palette, then go to **Select > Inverse**. Click on the layer mask for the top trail layer and fill this with black.

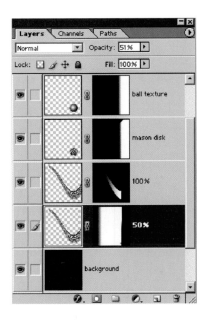

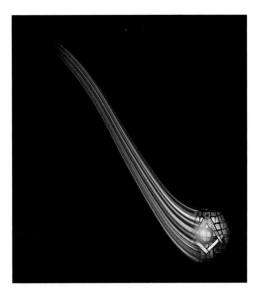

Text Brush effects

The text trail effect is fun and versatile, and there are surprisingly few steps to making it. These are: make a custom brush, create a path, and then stroke the path with your brush.

Text trail

5

Making the text brush

1. Type out a short piece of text in black.

2. Size matters for this effect, so change the size of the text (and the font), to approximately what you need. Too large is better than too small for this.

3. For any background layers behind the text, turn off the eye at the left side of the layers palette. The text should appear against a transparent background. Anything visible will be included in your new brush.

4. Enclose your text in a rectangular marquee selection.

5. **Edit > Define Brush** and give your new brush a name.

6. Drag the text layer to the trash can in the layers palette, and turn the eye back on for the background layer. CTRL-D to deselect.

If you make your brush in a lighter color than black, it will paint with a pale replica of the brush tip, and not with its full strength, even when you've set the brush opacity to 100%.

Creating the path

You can create a path that is simple or ornate, but for a text trail, you will probably have better results using a simple path. I describe here how to make the gentle curve in this example:

1. Type P to choose your Pen tool.

2. Click it at the beginning of where you want your path to start and then again at the end.

3. Choose the Convert Point tool from under your pen tool, in the toolbox.

4. Click the Convert Point tool on one of the endpoints and drag out the Bezier handle.

5. By pulling this handle around, you change the curve. Do the same with the other endpoint, if you want the line curved at that end, too.

5

Stroking the path

Keep in mind that, before you stroke a path, you have to remind Photoshop of which brush you want to use. If you do not define your brush, Photoshop will stroke it with an icky choppy black line!

1. Make a new layer. Be sure that it is active (clicked) in the Layers palette, and that it is visible.

2. Choose the Brush tool (type the letter B).

3. In your Brushes palette, carefully choose your options. For the smooth trail effect, in the Brush Tip Shape, set spacing to 1%. For a plain-color trail, all other options should be off.

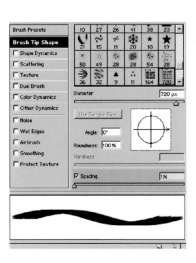

To set attributes for the Brush Options, you click on the name of the attribute on the left side of the Brush Options palette, and the options for that attribute will appear on the right.

4. Choose your desired color in the Color Picker.

5. Click the tab for the Paths palette and you should see your path there. Click on it to make it active.

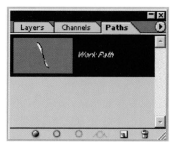

6. Click on the Stroke Path button at the bottom of the Paths palette.

7. Change colors and put a single click with your brush at the end of the trail. This made the black "Trade Secrets" you can see in the image here.

Copyright signature brush

This is really just an application of a special text brush, and is something that you might find useful.

1. Just as above, make your text. In this case, you may want to sign your name. Be sure to do it on a new layer.

   ■ To make ©, use the numeric keypad, hold down the ALT key and type 0169.

   ■ OPTION-G makes the © for Mac, also, OPTION-2 for ™ and OPTION-R for ®

   ■ On a laptop, you have to turn on NUMLK and be careful not to use the 0 from the regular keyboard, but the 0 at the bottom.

2. Turn off any background layers.

3. Make a rectangular selection around the signature and copyright information.

4. Go to **Edit > Define Brush**. Ctrl/Cmd+D to deselect.

5. When you are ready to sign your art, choose a color, and resize your brush with the keyboard modifiers] and [.

6. Put the signature on its own layer so you can move it around or use a layer effect on it. In this image, I've added my signature to a piece I digitally painted.

5

In this version, I raised the signature a bit with a little inner bevel.

Great textures

Making a realistic oak texture

Before we start with this wood, let me stress that any natural texture is inherently irregular. If you have too much regularity or uniformity, you lose the realism. Therefore, DON'T use my exact settings!

Making textures is a very forgiving process. Just about any color and filter combination can give you something that is remarkable; so don't hesitate to go a little crazy with this.

Oak is characterized by its distinctive grain. Its grain lines are considerably darker than its background. What we will do here is to paint "hairy" lines on the background for the main grain lines. Then we will distort them to give the bend of the grain. Adding some noise and a blur finishes the grain. Let's make some wood!

5

> **Hexadecimal codes:** *Hex codes for colors are the 6-digit numbers which you see at the bottom of your color picker. There are letters there, too, but those are actually numbers too! Here's why:*
>
> *The hexadecimals are actually 3 sets of two-digit numbers. The first two digits are for red; the second are for green; and the third are for blue. Each number is in base 16. That is where the "hexadecimal" comes from. You don't have to be able to do any conversions or math in order to use the hex codes.*
>
> *If you get into the habit of using the hexadecimal codes for the colors, you will reap more than one reward. First, when you do web editing, you will be using hex codes. And secondly, hex codes are much easier to remember than those cumbersome RGB codes. For example, compare #CAB555 to R 202, G 181, B 85.*
>
> *But actually, the hex codes are just a tidy way of defining R, G, and B! For example, #0000FF is nothing but blue. #FF0000 is nothing but red. I'll leave it to you to figure out what #00FF00 is. It is helpful to know that when all three sets of 2 are the same, you are dealing with a shade of gray. #000000 is black. #FFFFFF is white. #777777 is a medium gray.*

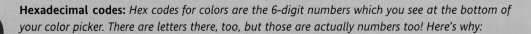

1. For this oak, you can begin with a background of grayed yellow, #CCBB77. To get this color, open your Color Picker and type the number into the # box. This is the hexadecimal code.

> *In the Color Picker make sure that the Only Web Colors box is left unchecked*

2. Go to **File > New**... Make it 300ppi and whatever size you want. Name the file 'oak'.

3. CTRL/CMD+SHIFT+N to make a new layer and click ALT+BACKSPACE to fill the layer with your foreground color of #CCBB77.

4. Now make your foreground color a yellowed brown, such as #554400.

5. Choose a wide, soft brush, of about 34 pixels, that will leave stray trails of paint. This default brush works well.

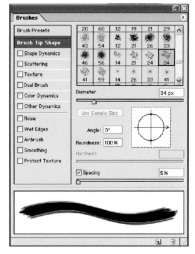

6. Paint some vertical lines on your canvas. Do not strive for perfection here! These will be your main grain lines for your oak.

7. **Filter > Distort > Shear**... and pull your line till it is something like a sine wave. This will make nice tight waves in your wood's grain. Click OK when you are done.

8. If you want to make your lines more steeply wavy, as I have done here, repeat the last filter with CTRL/CMD+F

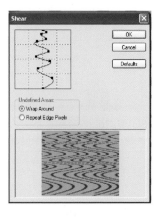

9. Go to **Filter > Noise > Add Noise**. Make it Monochromatic, Gaussian, and about 25%.

10. Then go to **Filter > Blur > Motion Blur**. Use an angle of 0°, with a distance of around 25–50 pixels. The distance will depend upon your screen resolution and the size of your image.

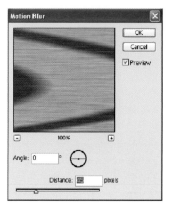

5

11. Go to **Image > Rotate Canvas** and give it a 90° rotation (either way).

12. CTRL+A to select your canvas, or if this wood is just one layer of your project, select the relevant layer. Click CTRL/CMD+T for Free Transform, RIGHT/CTRL-click to see the drop down menu, and choose **Rotate 90° CW.**

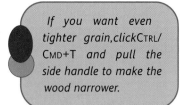

If you want even tighter grain, click CTRL/CMD+T and pull the side handle to make the wood narrower.

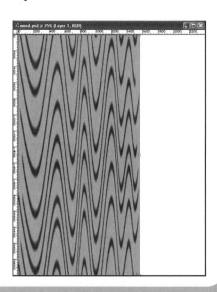

13. Go to **Filter > Noise > Add Noise** again. The same settings as before are fine.

We will blur this again, but this time, we pull the angle off just a bit. This little trick is what gives this oak its realism.

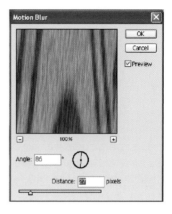

If you want to keep this texture to use later, follow these steps:

14. Crop your file so that there are no straggly edges and everything on your canvas is good oak, then click CTRL/CMD+S to save.

Flatten the document at this point. (**Layer > Flatten Image**). If it asks you, choose to discard any invisible layers. Set up a textures folder for all such files, and save the image. Go to **File > Save As** and save it in your new textures folder.

Press CTRL/CMD+F to re-apply the same filter with the same settings, and CTRL/CMD+ALT+F to re-open the last filter but adjust the settings.

Making a pattern from the oak

In a minute, we will use this oak to make its own layer style. To do this, we need to make the texture into a pattern. Here's how to make a pattern from the oak:

1. Drag a rectangular marquee selection around the part of the canvas that you want to be in your pattern. Make sure that everything inside the rectangular marquee is oak. For this oak pattern, use as much of the oak as you can.

Remember that anything inside your selection will be in your pattern, so turn off the eye for any unneeded layers. (For example, if you are doing TV lines, you want the background layer to be invisible, so you would turn off its eye.)

2. Go to **Edit > Define Pattern**, and then name your pattern something clever like "Oak" — simple! The pattern will now be available as a Pattern Overlay in the Layer Styles window.

Carved Wood: Using the Oak to make a banner

This procedure can be used with any texture. What we will do is open the texture file and cut out the shape we want. Then we will add some layer styles to make it look like a solid piece of wood, and finally "carve" our title into the banner:

5

1. Open your oak texture. If the texture image is not flattened, you should flatten it now.

2. You can modify your original texture a little by using an Adjustment Layer to tweak the color. Here the oak has a stained effect. If you don't want to adjust your image, then you need to create a new working layer now.

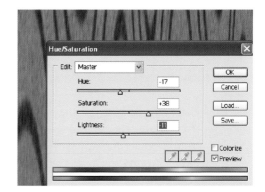

3. Now we are going to make the shape for the banner itself. Start by selecting the Shape tool from the toolbar.

4. In the Options bar choose the Rounded Rectangle tool and the Paths button. Set the Radius as appropriate, this will depend upon your screen resolution and how big you want your shape.

5. Drag out your shape.

Holding SHIFT as you drag out a shape will either constrain it to a uniform shape, or, in the case of a line or polygon, it will constrain its rotation to increments of 45°. Release your SHIFT key after you release your mouse.

6. Go to the Paths palette. Click the Load Path as Selection button at the bottom of that palette.

7. CTRL/CMD+SHIFT+I to Invert the selection.

8. Click the DELETE key on the keyboard to clear away everything but your shape.

Alternatively you could keep the entire texture, place it on a layer above the shape and use a Layer Clipping Group to offer more flexibility and options.

Working with Layer Styles

1. Click the **Add a layer style** button at the bottom of the Layers palette, and for this wood banner select **Bevel and Emboss** from the drop down menu.

2. Choose an **Inner Bevel**, and select **Chisel Hard** in the **Technique** field.

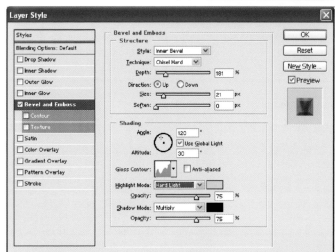

3. The default white highlight seems to give a bit of a plastic feeling, so change the highlight color to #FFCC99, with its mode set to **Hard Light**.

4. Certainly, experiment with the layer style combinations! You can specify not only bevels, drop shadows, and glows, but also stroke (outlining an object with a color, gradient, or pattern), gradient or pattern overlay, or blending options.

5

Saving Layer Styles

1. In the Layer Styles window Click the words **Pattern Overlay**. In the drop-down menu you should find the oak pattern, which you made above, add this to your layer style.

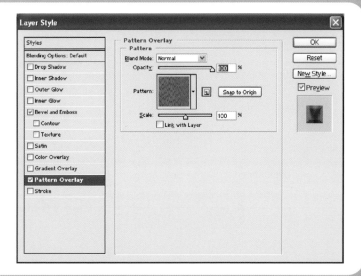

2. Once you are happy with your effect, if you decide you'd like to use it again with other layers, then you can save the layer style. Click the **New Style** button on the Layer Style dialog box.

3. Give your style a name, like 'Beveled Oak'.

In your Styles Palette (**Window > Styles** if it's not visible), you will see your new style there, at the bottom of the list. To use your style for any layer, have the layer selected in the Layers palette and click the box for that style in the Styles palette.

Anything you make in that layer will be chiseled out of oak! This includes filled shapes, text, and brush strokes!

Saving Styles

Each time you save a layer style, it will pop up in the Styles palette. If, however, you choose to reset your Styles palette then your new style will be lost. Fortunately you can save a set of styles for use at a later date. Here's how:

- Click the arrow in the top right of the Styles palette

- Click Save

- Find a good place for your styles and name the file something you will remember

5

Metallic effects

For this effect, you will make an Alpha Channel and use it to define your texture. Then, you will shine a light through this texture onto your layer, leaving you with hammered silver.

Using Alpha Channels for 3D Effects

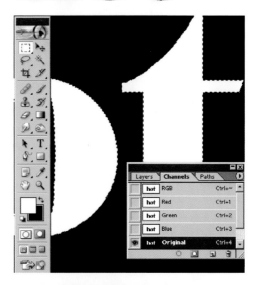

1. Type your text on a layer.

2. If you have to change the font or size, do so now, in the Text Options bar. Then CTRL/CMD+click the type layer to make it a selection.

3. Click on the Channels tab.

4. Click the Create a new Channel icon at the bottom of the Channels palette.

5. ALT-BACKSPACE to fill your selection with white (foreground color).

6. Double-click the name of the channel and rename it "Original."

*You **can** type directly into the Alpha channel, but it is not advisable as you are very limited in what editing you can do that way. If you do type it directly into the Alpha channel, it will look like this.*
Then click on the channel in the Channels palette and the text becomes a selection. Fill this with white and continue.

7. Drag the Original channel to the Create a New Channel icon to duplicate it.

8. To add some texture to this channel go to **Filter > Noise > Add Noise**. The amount of noise will depend upon how many "holes" you want in your silver. I used 15%.

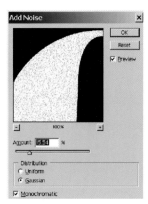

9. Filter > Pixelate > Crystallize... Your cell size will vary depending upon your screen resolution and how big you are doing your image. For mine, I used 19. If you are making Hammered or Hot Silver, use whatever it takes to get a similar result to this one.

10. Filter > Blur > Gaussian Blur. Again, this setting will depend upon your own resolution. I used 3.2.

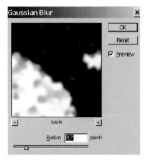

11. Rename this channel "Texture."

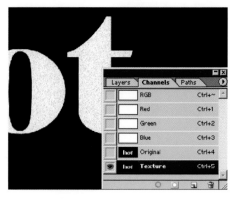

12. CTRL/CMD+click the Original channel to load it as a selection.

13. CTRL/CMD+SHIFT+I to invert the selection. Click the DELETE key on your keyboard. This trims any whiteness from the outside of your text. CTRL/CMD+D to deselect.

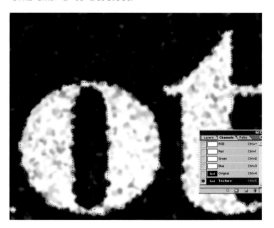

14. Prepare your layer, filling it with whatever color or texture you want.

Hammered silver

For making silver, I like to start out with #888888. For gold, my favorite start is usually #BEAD90. Silver and gold though, are really defined by the light that shines upon them.

1. Click on your Layers tab and click the Add a New Layer icon at the bottom of this palette.

2. For Hammered Silver, fill the layer with a neutral gray. Any sort of fill can be used for this kind of technique, though, and the results are very often surprisingly cool!

Bear in mind that lighting effects can be very draining on your RAM, and therefore have a knock on affect on Photoshop's performance. Be prepared for any crashes by saving your work before dealing with the lighting.

3. Go to **Filter > Render > Lighting Effects**. Choose Texture for Texture Channel. Choose Metallic, shiny, and Mountainous. Use the default light.

4. Drag your light in the dialog box around, till you like the effect. I like light coming from the upper left, because we are used to seeing things lit that way.

5. Trim the text on the layer, and return to the Channels palette. CTRL/CMD-click the Original channel to load it as a selection.

6. Return to the Layers palette and click your working layer in the palette. CTRL/CMD-SHIFT-I to invert the selection. Click the DELETE key on your keyboard.

7. Here is the Hammered Silver.

Erasing the hard-line edges, as in this image, makes it look more like naturally cast silver.

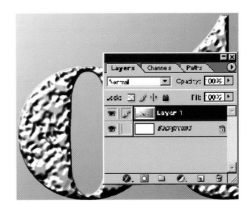

5

Hot Silver

Hot cast silver, fresh from the smelter! To get this look, we begin with Hammered Silver (just above). Then we will "melt" the silver! We're aiming for a red-hot, just-out-of-the-smelter look.

5

1. Zoom in until you can see the color differentiations well.

2. With contiguous turned off and the tolerance set to 5 or so, tap your magic wand to one of the black "valley" areas on your texture.

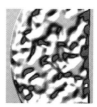

3. Make a new layer. Choose a bright red color, ALT-BACKSPACE to fill the selection with this color.

4. To make that glowing look, go to **Filter > Blur > Gaussian blur** ... to taste.

Getting a better glow

You can usually get a better glow by using multiple layers with different blurred colors. Make each successive selection a bit smaller than the last.

Scaling layer styles

Layers styles are great, but they have one major drawback - they are not resolution independent. This means that a style that was created on a certain image and resolution will not necessarily look good on another image.

With an almost hidden option to the layer effects, we can make the difference between the appearance of simply attaching a layer style or crafting a tasteful effect to our image.

1. To start with, I created some text and two butterfly images, using the custom shapes.

2. Each element is on a separate layer.

3. I added a default layer style to the text by selecting the text layer and clicking on one of the style thumbnails. Interesting look, but it's a bit ugly.

5

4. I applied layer styles to both the butterfly layers too.

Here is the trick:

5. Select one of the layers, here I chose the text layer. RIGHT/CTRL-click on the word "effects" and choose "scale effects" from the drop down menu.

6. A dialog box will appear. Adjust the size to suit. Notice how much better the style looks, now it is the correct size for the text. The scale layer effects will scale all the effects applied to layer proportionately.

7. Choose a butterfly layer and do the same thing. Notice the improvement.

8. Finally scale the last butterfly and you will see how much better our image looks. It looks a lot more professional.

5

Quick background zoom effect

This is one of my favorite effects for an instant background.

1. Hit D to reset the foreground and background colors.

2. Choose the background; go to **Filter > Render > Clouds**. This sets the base for our zoom effect.

3. Apply a radial blur, **Filter > Blur > Radial Blur**.

4. Use the zoom setting as shown in the screen capture.

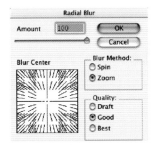

Here is the result. We will now add a color to it.

5. Go to **Image > Adjustments > Hue/Saturation**, and click the **Colorize** box.

6. Move the hue to select a color. Push the saturation up to saturate the color or make it more intense. Here we have chosen a nice golden color.

5

Making objects with layer styles glassy

We are going to take the same image we created in the scale layer style tip.

For this effect to work, you will need at least one object with layer styles applied. At the very least we will need a bevel style on the layer.

To achieve the transparent effect, we are going to hide the actual image and be left with the layer style only. In order for the effect to work, turn off any color overlay effects. Click the eye next to the individual effect.

In the Layers palette you will have noticed the addition of a new **Fill** opacity setting in Photoshop 7.

1. Reduce the fill opacity to 0. The fill is the actual image. The top opacity setting is the master. The fill opacity doesn't affect the layer effects.

   Notice the nice glassy look to the text. There is still a translucent purple color (because the highlight in the bevel is set to purple and not white – set it to white for a full transparent effect) But I like the effect so let's keep it.

2. Choose the remaining layers and adjust the fill opacity to 0 respectively.

3. Be sure to turn off any overlay effects. Here we turned off the color overlay and pattern overlay.

The result is a nice glassy look.

Experiment with the tip for some really cool glass and liquid effects.

5

Getting burned

It is said that those of us who do image manipulation always want what we do not have: We want photos to look like paintings, and paintings to look like photos. If it is old, we want it to look new. If it is new, we want it to look old. And sometimes we want to burn it!

Cutting away the burned edge

For this image you will need an image that you want to set on fire, if you don't have an appropriate image, then you can download this paper image from the friends of ED web site.

1. RIGHT/CTRL-click the paper layer to load the layer as a selection. We'll then subtract from this selection by holding ALT whilst making further selections.

2. Type L for your Lasso tool and then, holding ALT, draw a rough edge around the part you want cut out.

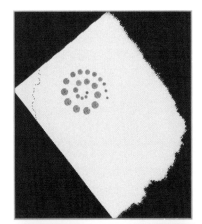

3. Click the Add Layer Mask button at the bottom of the Layers palette, the roughly drawn selection will now be gone.

In this way, you are able to restore this cut area, if you want to, by deleting or repainting the layer mask. The layer mask also gives you a ready selection of the paper, as you are about to see.

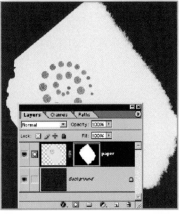

Early-burn layer

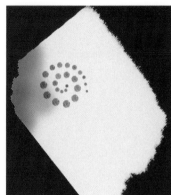

1. Select the paper by CTRL/CMD+ clicking the layer mask, and then make a new layer above the paper layer.

2. Choose a wide soft brush, no dynamics, 50% opacity and 50% flow, and pick an orange-brown for the foreground color. (Mine is #AC804E.)

3. Paint the early-burn. Be sure that you completely cover the edge and be a bit erratic. This is, after all, fire!

4. At the top of the Layers palette, change the blending mode of this layer to Multiply or Linear Burn, especially if you have something written on the paper, or if it is a photo.

5

Charred layer

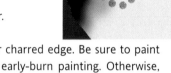

1. Leave the same selection active, CTRL/CMD+SHIFT+N to make a new layer.

2. Press D followed by X to set black as the foreground color.

3. Using the same brush as in the early-burn layer, paint your charred edge. Be sure to paint thoroughly along the burned-away edge. Stay within the early-burn painting. Otherwise, don't strive for evenness. CTRL/CMD+D to deselect.

Fire!

This is not one of those one-step fire effects, and while I wouldn't want to set a whole line of text alight using this effect, it is good for a realistic single flame. It is done almost completely without filters, just a bit of Gaussian blur and a bit of Liquify.

1. Begin by making a selection around the approximate area where you want your flame. In the Options bar, set Feather to 5 or so. (This will vary depending upon the size of your image and its resolution.) The goal is a bit of glow and not a sharp edge.

2. Now you will paint several layers, each using a different color. The colors I have used are listed here as the layer names, but there is NOT anything magical about these. The only one that is important is that the top one should be painted in #FFFFFF, which will give you the white-hot center of your flame.

   After you get all of the layers, you can blur them individually or reduce opacity if you need to, because each of the colors is on its own layer.

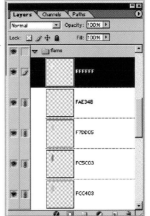

3. Now take the Smudge tool, and beginning with a broad brush and a Strength setting of about 25%, I smudged upward, forming the flame. Start with the bottom layer and work upwards, doing the #FFFFFF last. CTRL/CMD+D to deselect. (You can deselect before this step, too.)

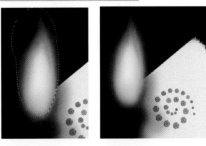

5

4. Here the base seems too broad, so link all of the layers and then go **Edit > Transform > Distort** gave the following result.

5. A great match flame, but doesn't look like the paper is burning. With a light touch on **Filter > Liquify**, pull the bottom flame down into thin "legs".

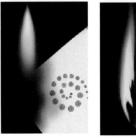

Making effects is one of the most creative uses of Photoshop, and as always lots of experimentation will yield fantastic results. Throughout this chapter we've seen some of the tools and techniques that Photoshop offers to create stunning effects.

Many people assume that Photoshop special effects are all about layer styles, and although they do play an important role, we've seen here that there are many effects that can be created through clever use of Transform options, Layer Masks, paths and customized brushes, and more.

The trick is to use these tools and techniques imaginatively, be inspired by objects and colors around you, and most of all have fun experimenting.

Web banners

Animated banners

The Web Gallery feature

Creating an entire web site in Photoshop

6: Web Graphics

Over the past few years Photoshop has become a real player in the web graphics world. With the release of ImageReady a few years back, some very powerful tools became available to designers. In recent years Photoshop and ImageReady have become more and more attuned to the needs of the web design community, and it is now possible to create fantastic sites almost entirely in Photoshop and ImageReady. In this chapter we'll do just that, using the new features which appeared with Photoshop 7, as well as some tried and tested secrets to getting your images on the web and making them move, load quickly, and interact with the user's mouse movements.

Web banners

As a designer, sooner or later in your career you are going to be asked to create a web banner. We'll go through each step of the process, showing the best shortcuts and fully exploiting the new features of Photoshop 7.

Use preset sizes

Photoshop 7 now has preset document sizes built into it.

1. Create a new file, and when the New dialog box opens, choose the web banner option from the preset sizes drop-down.

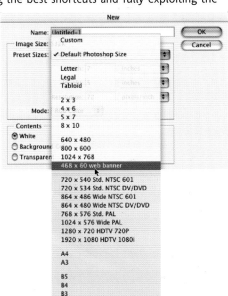

Web safe colors

Lets create a background fill for the banner.

1. Open the color picker by double-clicking on the color swatch on the toolbar. You will see an option on the bottom left, **Only Web Colors**.

2. Click this to limit the color picker to the 216 web safe colors. These are the colors that are consistent across all platforms.

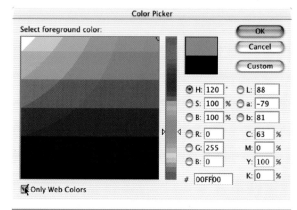

6

3. Create some text to go on the banner. Here is a very simple banner, advertising a rather fantastic Photoshop book!

Save for Web

Let's save this image for the web. Rather than just save it, we are going to optimize it. This means that we are going to reduce its final document size so that it loads quickly on the Internet. The Save for Web feature in Photoshop is really excellent for this, and throughout this section we will look at some of its features.

1. Go to **File > Save for Web...**

Optimize to File Size

Your image will open in the Save for Web screen, and the first thing we want to get right here is file size. Often when you submit a banner to a site, they will have rules including a maximum file size. I remember in Photoshop 4 and 5 playing around with my image, changing colors and removing elements to get it down to an acceptable size. Fortunately, there is now a great feature introduced in Photoshop 6 called **Optimize to File Size**.

1. Click on the little arrow next to settings and choose **Optimize to File Size**.

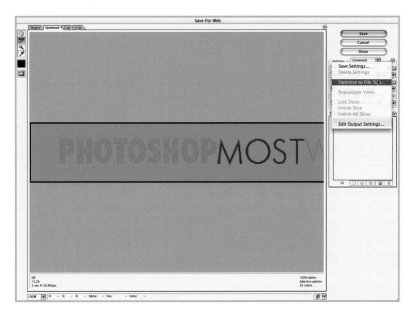

2. The important setting here is the **Desired File Size**. Enter a number here and Photoshop will attempt to compress your image until it reaches the specified size. Usually it's good to set it to **Auto Select GIF/JPEG** and let Photoshop do its work and decide what format will compress the best.

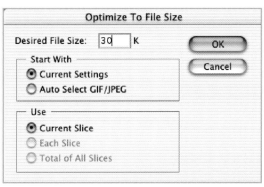

6

Here is the result, a GIF file with the palette reduced to the necessary colors.

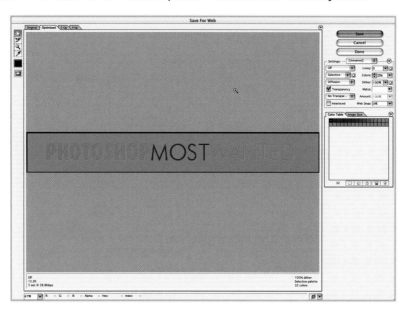

3. Click Save and choose where to save your image. It will save a copy of the optimized image.

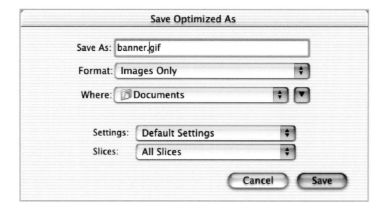

Important points

- Always save an uncompressed and unflattened version of your image in PSD form in case you need to make changes later.

- Never make changes to a GIF or a JPG, and resave as they will be twice compressed and lose too much quality.

- Always resave the uncompressed image.

Animated banners

ImageReady 7, which ships as part of Photoshop 7, includes tools for doing advanced web processing of images, as well as for creating web animations and rollovers. With the image open in Photoshop, lets take it to ImageReady now so we can create a simple animation

Switching applications

Press the bottom-most button on the tool bar; this is the **Jump to ImageReady** button. ImageReady has a similar button for switching to Photoshop in the same location.You can also use **File > Jump To > ImageReady**, CTRL/CMD+SHIFT+M.

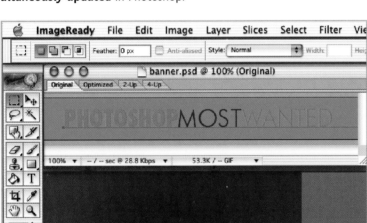

After a little pause, ImageReady will launch with our image loaded up. The image will still be active in Photoshop and when you make changes in ImageReady, they will be **simultaneously updated** in Photoshop.

6

Animation

At the bottom of the screen you'll see the Animation palette, (if it's not visible go to **Window > Animation**). You will notice a thumbnail of our image with a number 1 in the top left corner of the animation palette. This indicates the frame number – ImageReady will make a series of frames that will change, simulating motion. Each of these frames will be embedded into a graphics file called an **animated GIF**. These enhanced GIFs actually contain multiple images, that we call the frames.

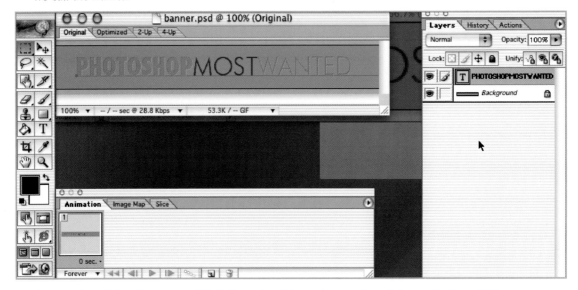

Our aim here is for the text to slide in from the right and stop where it is now in the middle.

1. Select the text layer and using the Move tool, drag the text all the way to the right and just off the image. Hold the SHIFT key to constrain the horizontal baseline.

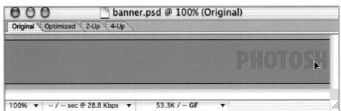

2. Click on the **Duplicate current frame** button at the bottom of the Animation palette. Unsurprisingly, this will make a duplicate of frame 1, called frame 2.

6

With frame 2 selected in the Animation palette, drag the layer until it is in the center. Don't forget to hold down the SHIFT key.

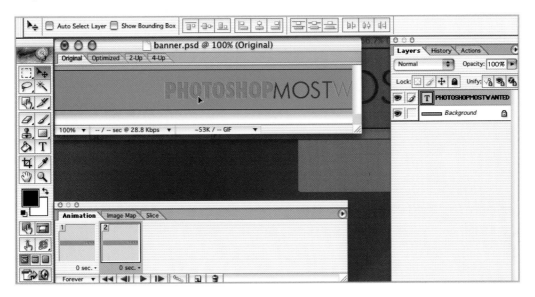

We now have a 2-frame animation. If we play it the image will jump backward and forward. What we need to do is create some in-between frames that will smooth the animation. We could create new frames and just move the text a little bit on each, but once again the good folk at Adobe have added another great feature called **tweening**. Tweening is short for "in-be*tweening*". It used to be the job of junior animators to create the tween frames on the movies while the masters did all the creative work. ImageReady serves as the junior animator and you as the master can tell it how many frames you need and they will be created for you in the twinkling of an eye.

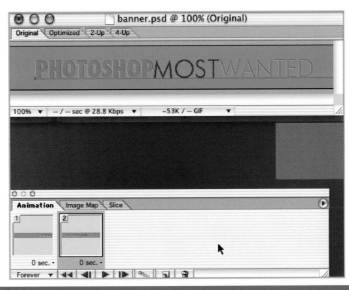

3. Click on the drop-down at the top right of the Animation palette and choose **Tween...**

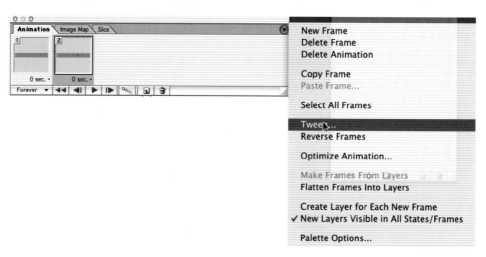

6

Tweening

We now have some options. **Tween With** allows us to choose to either tween with the previous or the next frame. Since we want the tween frames in between our active and previous frames we will choose **Previous Frame**. In the **Frames to Add** field select 5.

The **Layers** options will allow you to animate multiple layers together or just select the active layer. In our case it won't hurt to keep it on the default **All Layers** since there is only one. If the **Selected Layer** option is checked, then the tweening will only be applied to whichever layer is currently active.

The **Parameters options let us choose whether to** animate **Position**, **Opacity**, or **Effects** of the image. In most cases you would want to animate all three aspects, but should you be trying to achieve a particular effect, then you can deselect the relevant parameter

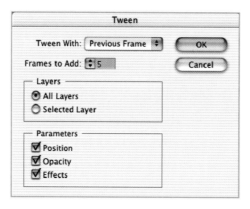

4. Press OK and our little hidden animation assistant will create all the frames for us resulting in a smooth motion animation.

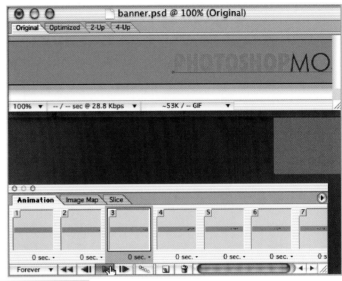

There is just one problem with the animation now. It keeps repeating so fast that there is barely time to read the message. What we need to do is add a pause at the end of the animation before it loops. Easy, under each frame is a delay; the default is set to 0.

5. Select the last frame and click the tiny arrow to access a menu. Change the delay to 5 seconds. This will cause the animation to pause for 5 seconds before repeating the loop.

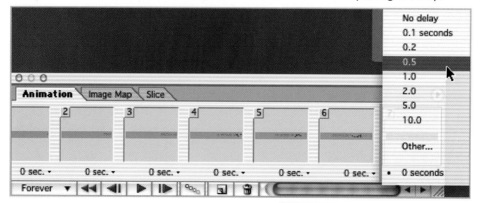

6

> *To add the same delay to all frames, click on the first frame, then SHIFT and click on the last frame and right/CTRL-click to add the required amount of delay.*

Previewing in a web browser

You can either preview your animation in ImageReady, by clicking the **Preview Document** button or simply clicking Y. However, it is a good idea to see what your animation will look like on the web. Click CTRL/CMD+ALT+P to preview in a web browser. Animations will often run faster and smoother in a web browser than in ImageReady.

Your web browser will be launched, and your animation will go through its paces with all the relevant information displayed under it.

To save your animation, go to **File > Save Optimized**, or click CTRL/CMD+ALT+S.

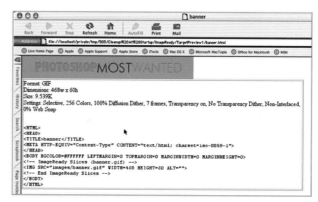

Save for Web revisited

Now we'll take a more detailed look at the Save for Web option, and see what we can do with it without ever leaving Photoshop. The save for web option is a mini application within in Photoshop and it's loaded with features, we'll run through some of them now. To access the Save for Web dialog go to **File > Save for Web**. Or use the shortcut ALT+SHIFT+CTRL/CMD+S.

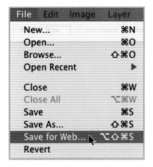

The idea is to work out the best settings for retaining quality whilst aiming for a small file size. The tabs at the top of the window allow you to compare the different versions of your image.

- **Original** shows your image without compression.

- **Optimized** is the highest quality compression, it is likely to still have a high file size.

- **2-Up** allows you to compare the original and the optimized versions.

- **4-Up** displays the original and 3 different optimized images together for comparison.

6

Notice that our image is being displayed in GIF format, for photos or other images with gradients and blends, JPEG is usually a better file format. This is because GIF has limited colors, and will display such images with bands of colors instead of the smooth gradations of color you want. For this photo-realistic example we want our image to be a JPEG, so go to the Settings panel and select **JPEG** in the drop-down menu.

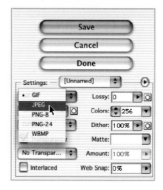

This changes the selected preview to a JPEG, but the other two remain as GIFs.

To change all previews to JPEGs, click the little arrow next to the Settings options. In the drop-down palette choose **Repopulate Views**. This will automatically change the other two optimized previews to the selected mode.

Notice how the optimization settings decrease in steps of roughly 50% from the selected preview: We started with a quality setting of 55, the next preview is at 27, and the final one at 13.

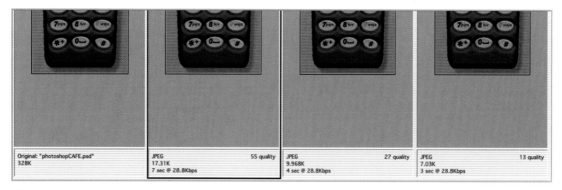

If we wanted to see previews at a higher setting we could go to the Settings panel, and set the Quality setting to, say, 81. We'd then need to hit Repopulate Views again, and Photoshop would generate two new optimizations, with higher quality settings, in this case 35 and 20.

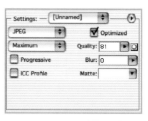

6

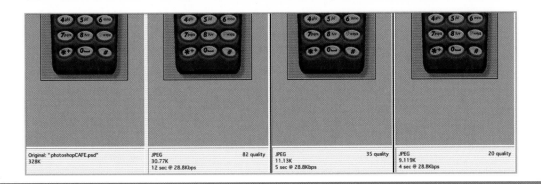

| Original: "photoshopCAFE.psd"
328K | JPEG
30.77K
12 sec @ 28.8Kbps | 82 quality | JPEG
11.13K
5 sec @ 28.8Kbps | 35 quality | JPEG
9.119K
4 sec @ 28.8Kbps | 20 quality |

Become a file size miser

We now have to work out what is the lowest we can possibly make our file size we can afford to have without sacrificing too much of the image quality.

The lowest quality image seems to be okay, but if you look closely, you see that we are beginning to lose a little of the image definition, the colors are not as clear, and the edges seem jagged. At 35, however, the image still looks good but the file is now only 11.78k. Compare that to the original, which weighs in at 326k and you can start to see why image optimization is so important.

Lets preview it in the web browser like we did in ImageReady, except the button is now located at the bottom right of the window.

Here is our image and all the data just like in ImageReady, but we are still in Photoshop!

6

Saving optimization settings

If you are working on a batch of images with similar resolution and content and you need to optimize them all, then once you are happy with the optimization settings for one image, you may wish to save your settings as a starting point for the others.

In the Settings drop-down, choose save **Save Settings**.

Here you can name your settings and save it as an **IRS** (**ImageReady setting**) file. Your settings will now appear in the Settings menu to be used at a later date.

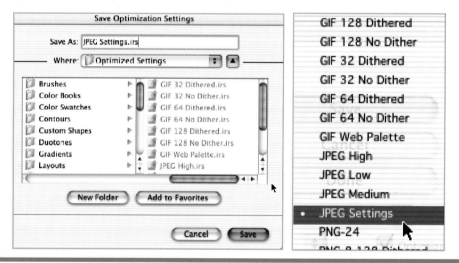

Adding a blur to reduce file size

Because of the way that JPEG compresses files, a blurred image will be smaller than a sharp one. When we select JPEG optimization there is a blur slider. If we really want to compress our images, we can add a slight blur to our image to tweak the last bit of optimization out of an image. Be careful not to blur too much or the image will be too degraded, add just enough until you start to notice it, then pull it back a notch or 2.

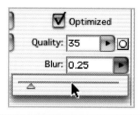

6

Here is our same image with a 0.25 blur added. This has knocked almost 10% off our file size. The file size is now 10.88k or 3 seconds on a 56k modem. Not bad for such a large detailed image.

Here is our original next to the optimized version.

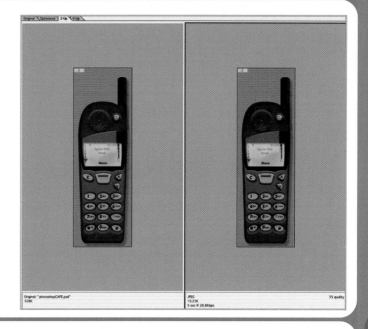

The Web Photo Gallery feature

A friend recently told me about how he'd put his vacation pictures on the web. He described how he carefully scanned them all into his computer. Then he explained the process of converting them all to the correct size and placing them into HTML pages. After that he had to make thumbnail previews out of all the images and put hyperlinks to each page. Not to mention the captions and the links on each page to go to the next and previous image. When he told me this, I cringed and was pained to tell him that Photoshop could have done all this for him in just a few minutes!

If you have ever built a gallery the long hard way, this section will cause you to either jump for joy or throw the book onto the floor in disgust. Whatever your reaction, your days of hard labor are finally over. Meet the **Web Photo Gallery** feature in Photoshop. All you need to start is a folder with your pictures in it. If you're lucky enough to have a digital camera, you won't even have to scan the pictures.

Creating a web gallery

We will walk though the process of creating your gallery step by step.

1. Launch the Web Photo Gallery, its located under **File** > **Automate** > **Web Photo Gallery**.

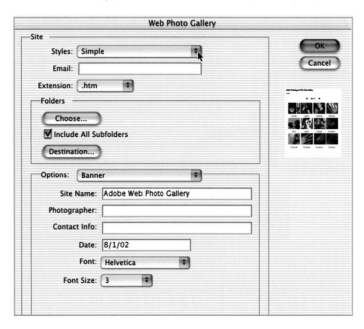

6

2. Choose the style of gallery you prefer, you can see a preview to the right. We have chosen Horizontal Blue and Gray. The process is the same no matter which style you choose.

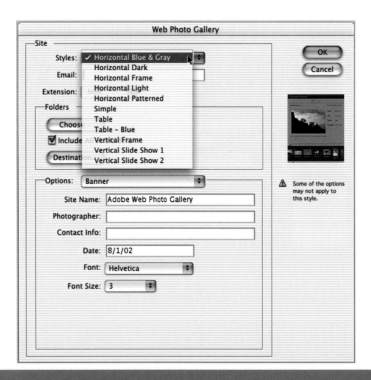

It doesn't matter if you use htm, or html as the extension. So don't worry about changing this.

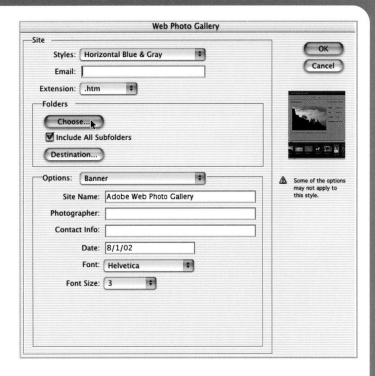

3. In the **Folders** section you can choose your image directory and define the destination directory to publish your gallery. Hit the **Choose** button (**Browse** if you are in Windows).

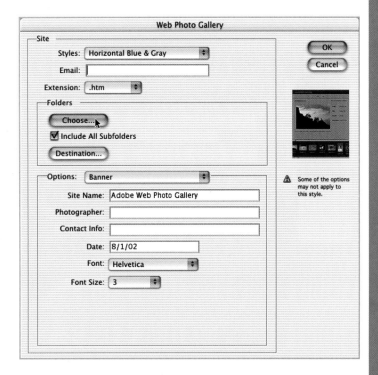

6

4. Navigate to your images folder where your photos are awaiting their big debut on the web.

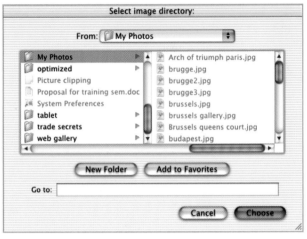

5. Uncheck **Include All Subfolders** unless you want Photoshop to drill down to every subdirectory in the folder looking for pictures. If this is the case, then leave it checked.

6. Click on **Destination**.

7. Create a new folder for your gallery. I called it "Web_Gallery", I always avoid spaces in my files names as they can cause problems on some Unix servers.

   Note: The new folder must be in a different directory to the source files.

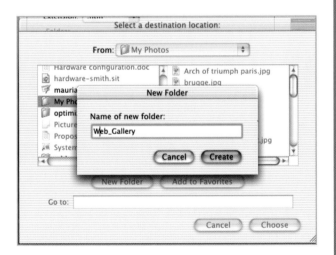

6

Now we are ready to move to the **Options** section of the dialog box.

Banner: This is where you can add the information that will go at the top of the page. You can name the page, and include the name of the photographer and contact information if you wish. By default the date is included, you can change the format or turn it off entirely.

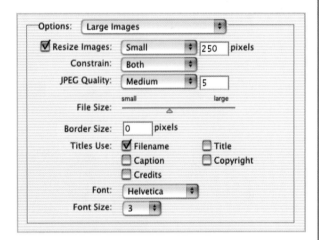

Large Images: These are the main images that will appear when the viewer clicks on the thumbnail. You can choose the final size and JPEG quality. The rest of the options are self-explanatory.

Thumbnails: Since these small representations of the images load faster than large images, you can scroll through them quickly and choose which images you would like to view full size. Here you can choose how large you would like them to be.

6

Custom Colors: Here you can change the colors of your gallery, these options are very self explanatory.

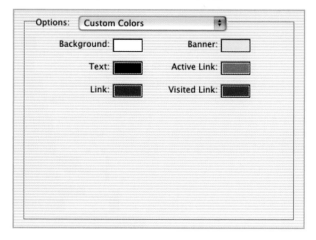

Security: This will help you to avoid people stealing your images and reusing them without your permission. We are now going to add a simple watermark to our images.

8. In the **Content** drop-down, select **Custom Text**, and type your name.

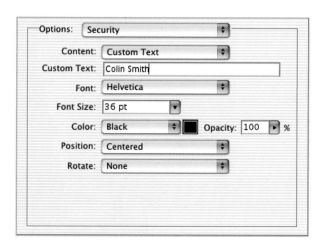

9. Move the Opacity slider down to around 30%. This will be enough for the text to be visible on the image without distracting from the image itself too much.

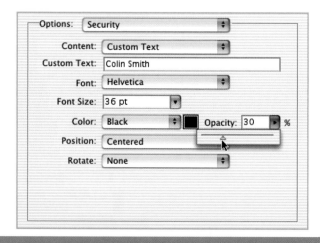

6

10. That's all the preparation done – now it's time to allow Photoshop to do some work for us. When you are satisfied with all your settings, click OK.

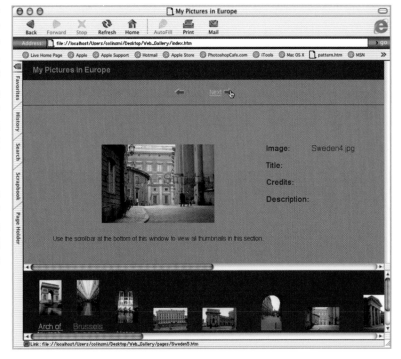

The time to create the gallery will vary depending on how many images Photoshop has to process and the size of the images. When the process is complete, your default web browser will launch with your finished gallery fully functional.

Feel free to click on the thumbnails and view your images. If you prefer, use the forward and backward arrows to view all the large images.

6

Notice the watermark? This is a great deterrent for would be image thieves.

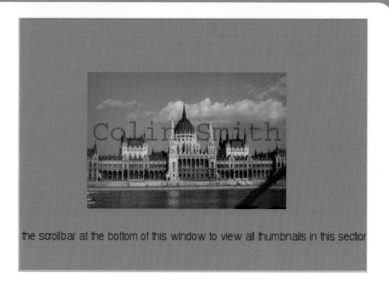

11. Now copy the entire directory you created the gallery in, and load it to your web server. To link your homepage to the gallery just add a link to the `index.htm` file.

Congratulations, now you can spend more time taking your photos, instead of slaving over thumbnails and HTML.

6

Creating an entire web site in Photoshop

Adding a navigation bar

We are going to use this web page for a fictitious band Hazardous Waste to learn a few techniques and tips. You can download this background image from the friends of ED website.

1. Starting with this image as the background, our first task will be to add a navigation bar.

2. Create a strip across the top of the page, and use the Eyedropper to sample a color from the page. This is a great way to match color.

3. Then, using another color, create a layer and make a rectangle, this will be our button.

4. Use a bevel and a drop shadow layer style to make the rectangle look more like a button. Layer styles work really well for rollover effects, as we will see later on in this chapter.

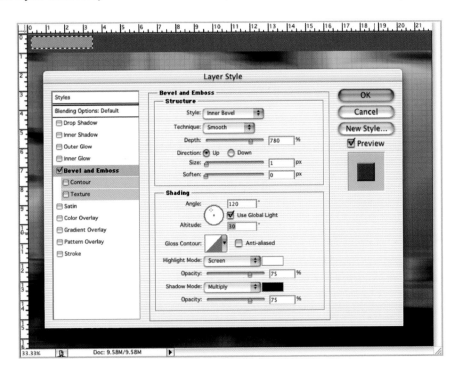

6

Duplicating layer elements

There is a super-easy way to duplicate layers. Just hold down the ALT key as you drag the object and Photoshop will create a duplicate of the object.

Keep duplicating until you have four buttons, don't worry about trying to line them up yet. I will show you a quick way.

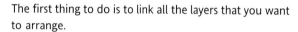

6

Align and distribute

We are going to get Photoshop to automatically space all the buttons and line them up.

The first thing to do is to link all the layers that you want to arrange.

Be sure you select the layer you want all of the other layers to align to before you begin to do this. Whichever layer is selected is the one the others will adjust their positions to match.

1. With the Move tool selected you will see the alignment tools at the top of the tool bar. Press the Align top button and all the objects will be lined up with the top edges.

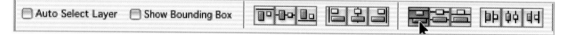

2. Now press the Distribute center button and all the objects will be evenly spaced.

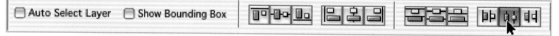

Anti-aliasing text

1. We're now going to add some text to the buttons, select the Type tool, and choose Sharp as the anti-aliasing mode in the Options bar.

Anti-aliasing *refers to the method Photoshop uses to blend the edges of an object with the surrounding colors to give a smoother appearance. When creating text for the Web, you need to select* **Sharp** *as the anti-aliasing mode, as this keeps small text smooth without looking too blurry.*

2. It is important that the text for each button is put on a new layer, so that the rollovers will work correctly, Click on each button's layer in turn in the Layers palette, before typing. This will not only ensure each button name has its own layer, but also that they will be sat above the appropriate button in the Layers palette. This will help to avoid future confusion.

 It is a good idea to link each button layer to its text layer, so that if you do any rearranging or resizing, they will automatically stay together, without losing any editability.

Slicing for the Web

We'll now switch to ImageReady to slice the images. It is possible to do this in Photoshop, indeed the slicing features of Photoshop and ImageReady are identical, but I prefer to do my slicing in ImageReady.

So, why do we need to slice the images at all? The reasons for slicing are:

- To create rollover effects

- To make slices clickable areas

- Smaller images load faster than one big image

- You can optimize parts of the image as a GIF and other parts as JPEG

- You can animate small sections of an image

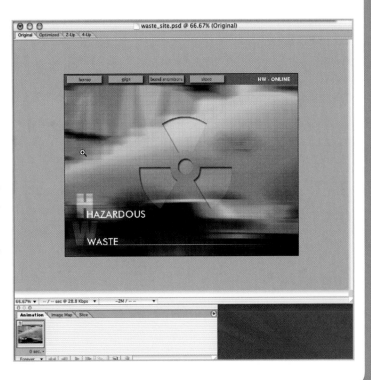

6

1. Before slicing, it is a good idea to optimize the whole image, to avoid having to change each slice individually. Go to the **Optimize** palette and select **JPEG Medium** in the Settings drop-down. (The convenience of the Optimize palette is one of the reasons I do my slicing in ImageReady.)

2. Click K to select the **Slice** tool, or go to the toolbox.

3. To create a slice just click and drag your mouse with the Slice tool selected. You will see a small square at the top left with a number in it. This is your slice. The image will be cut into smaller images along the lines and reassembled seamlessly in a table.

4. Draw a slice around another section of the image.

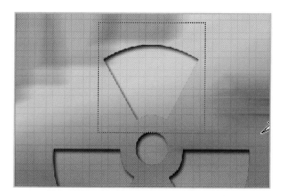

5. You'll see that ImageReady has created all the other slices for you.

6

6. Do this again a couple of times and notice how ImageReady creates all the slices that are needed automatically. This is too easy!

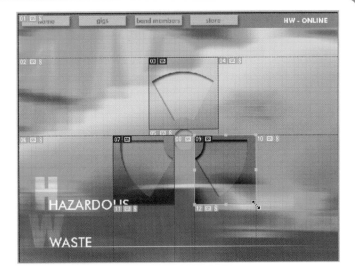

7. Now create a slice around each of the buttons.

8. Here is our image with all the slices applied.

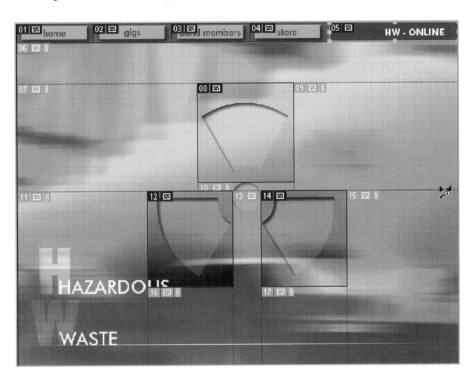

6

Moving slices

Don't worry if you put the slice in the wrong place, simply use the **Slice Select** tool to click on the slice and notice the bounding lines appear. It's now a simple matter to drag the slice boundary lines until you are satisfied that they line up correctly. If you prefer, you can just drag the entire slice to another area using this tool.

When choosing the Slice Select tool, note the small arrow at the bottom of the tool pop out menu. Clicking on this will remove the tool(s) from the tools menu and present them to you on a tiny separate palette.

Layer based slices

It is not ideal to move parts of our design around *after* we've cut everything up. This can make things a bit tricky. A great way to avoid all this extra work is to create **layer based slices**. Normally we will select our slices using a marquee, and then snap our slice lines to this marquee. With layer based slices, instead of using a marquee and slicing accordingly, we are going to slice using a layer as our guide.

Using **Layer > New Layer Based Slice** cuts out a lot of these steps. All we need to do is choose an appropriate layer and ImageReady will create a slice from it. The great part about using this technique is that if we later decide to move or resize the layer, ImageReady will alter the slice accordingly – a great timesaver.

Optimizing individual slices

The real power of ImageReady is the ability to optimize individual slices. Let's say we have an image of someone leaning against a white wall. What's the best optimization setting for this image – if we're concerned about file size that is?

The person will have lots of gradations of color, and so definitely be candidate for JPEG, but the wall, with it's flat color is GIF material. It would be a waste to have to save the entire image as JPEG, and if we save it as a GIF, the part where the person is will suffer from lack of color.

We can use slices to fix this problem. All we need to do is create a slice around the person, optimize this slice as a JPEG and then select the wall slices and optimize them separately as GIFs.

If we just slice our image up without paying attention to sizes we will actually increase the file size slightly – as each slice actually adds a little to the overall size. This is because each image we create has, amongst other things, a tiny identification header in it that tells your computer what file type it is.

When slicing, ask yourself whether creating the slice will reduce the file size more than not creating it. If it's a small area, the answer is: probably not. Check the size of the area before and then after the slice (by adding the file size of the two new areas together) if you're really worried about this.

Important points when optimizing

■ Areas of flat color don't need a lot of color detail, so are best suited to GIFs, which will give a much smaller file size.

■ Areas with gradients and lots of color optimize best with JPEGs.

■ You can optimize darker areas and areas with lots of changing color more heavily as it's less noticeable.

■ Fine and light areas show babble (where the image is changed from the original to a bad imitation, usually around the edges of objects) more readily.

6

*When you have been working with the Slice tool, even if you are on a different image for which you don't want slices, your image will have the little slice number in the upper left corner, denoting one slice. This can be very annoying! To get rid of that little number, click **View > Clear Slices**. If you want to maintain your slices, but do not want them to show, click **View > Show**... and uncheck Slices.*

Assigning links to the slices

1. Change to the Slice Select tool.

2. Whenever we click inside a slice with the Select tool, it will activate that slice and dim all the others. Select the first button.

3. In the **Slice** palette (nested with the Animation palette by default) type your link into the URL field. It should end with .html. This is the link that will be displayed when the user's mouse clicks in the slice.

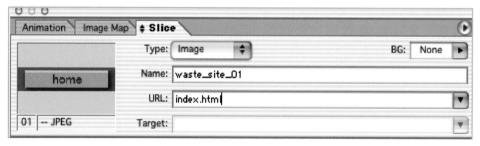

4. You can preview the page in a web browser and this is what it will look like.

Creating rollovers

JavaScript rollovers make an image change as the viewer rolls the mouse over part of them. Often the object is made to move or change color. To create a rollover, you need an original and also a new image for the rollover state, and then load both images into ImageReady. ImageReady will then write the JavaScript so that the two images are switched at the right moment.

1. Select a button.

2. Now open the **Rollovers** palette, (**Window > Rollovers** if it is not visible). You will notice that our slice is highlighted in the palette.

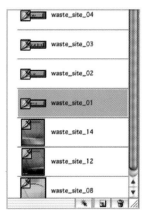

3. Press the **Create rollover state** button on the bottom of the palette.

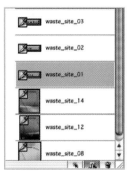

6

4. A new state will be created, called the **Over State**, meaning that the effect will be activated when the mouse moves over the slice.

5. Whatever you change in the Rollovers palette will be reflected in the rollover. The easiest way to make a change is to do something with the layer style. In this case let's click on the eye by the word Effects. This will turn off the layer effect when the mouse rolls over.

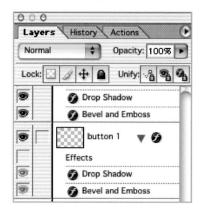

See how it will affect the image: it will make the button appear depressed. Now apply the rollover to each of the buttons.

6. Press the Preview button to test your rollover effect in ImageReady. When you move the mouse over the buttons they will change. Press the Preview button again to stop the effect.

6

Image Map

Just for fun, I am going to make a hidden button. When you click on the word "Waste" an e-mail will be sent to the owner of the website. We can define a clickable area by using an **Image Map**.

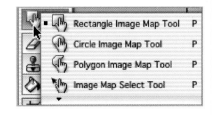

Click P to select the **Image Map** tool, there are several shapes available to make an image map. For the sake of this example, we will use the rectangle.

The Image Map tool works in a similar way to the Slice tool, simply click and drag to define an area. To create a hyperlink, type a URL into the Image Map palette. To set an e-mail link, type **mailto:** followed by an e-mail address.

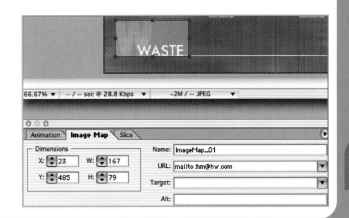

6

Hide and go seek

We can toggle the display of the image maps on and off with the Visibility button. Right next to it is a button to toggle the Slices Preview.

Optimizing images

One of the most powerful features of ImageReady is the ability to optimize whole images, as well as individual slices.

1. Click on the Optimized tab to view the optimized image preview.

2. Choose the Slice Select tool and choose one of the buttons.

3. Our buttons are made up of areas of flat color, so they should be optimized in GIF format. They will look best in this format, and the file size will be kept nice and low. Select GIF in the Optimize palette.

4. The parts of the image containing gradients and blends of color, will compress better as JPEGs. With these slices choose JPEG and lower the compression to a good balance of file size and quality, as we discussed earlier in the Save for Web discussion.

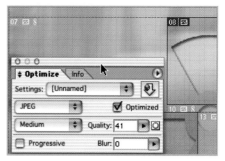

6

5. Now preview the page in a web browser by pressing the Preview in Web Browser button, which sits near the bottom of the tool bar. It's always a good idea to preview the effects of the file compression before committing to them.

Here is our page in the web browser, all the rollovers are working fine and the image looks good at the current optimization settings.

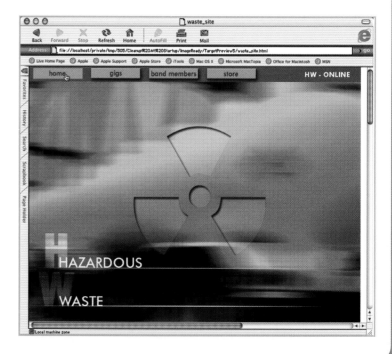

Exporting the page

To take all this work to the web just hit **File > Save Optimized As...**

Choose a location and a filename, ImageReady will then export the page with all the sliced images and create all the html and JavaScript for you.

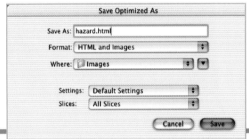

You can find all the elements of the web page in the exported folder. ImageReady has even created an images folder for you.

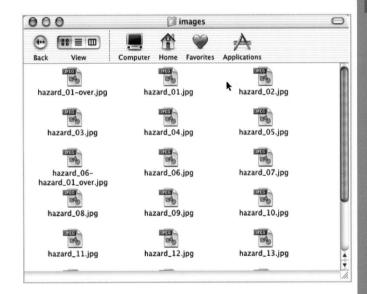

As we have seen, Photoshop and ImageReady simplify the process of building interactive and dynamic web pages. We have reviewed the creation of rollovers, optimization of images, image maps, and interactive rollovers, we have also shown how Photoshop makes it easy to create a web Photo gallery. The key is to harness the power of Photoshop to create some great visual web graphics.

6

Customizing Photoshop

Workspace

The Preferences window

Other settings

7: Setting up

Customizing Photoshop

An important part of working with Photoshop is making it your own – customizing the way Photoshop works to fit with your needs. This includes tweaking preferences, adjusting the Preset Manager, creating Tool Presets, making Custom Shapes, defining colors and making your own workspaces. In this chapter we'll look at how to use all of these customization features, and we'll then run through the options available in the Preferences menu, before rounding off with a canny way to create a shortcut for just about anything at all.

The Preset Manager

The **Preset Manager** controls the contents of the following palettes: Brushes, Swatches, Gradients, Styles, Patterns, Contours, Custom Shapes, and Tools. You can find it by going to **Edit > Preset Manager**.

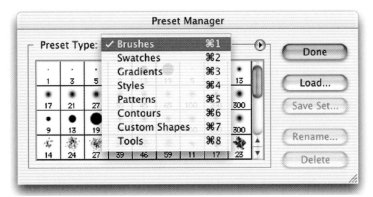

If you make a change in the Preset Manager, the display of these palettes will change. For example, if there are brushes you never use, you could delete them. Or, if you have created a series of brushes, and you want to make them a permanent part of the Brushes palette, you want to change the order of the brushes. All of these kinds of operations are done through the Preset Manager.

Creating a subset

Many people find that they use different types of brushes for different procedures – larger soft brushes for working with photographs, for example. It is possible to create smaller sets of brushes that you load when you need them. To make a new set of brushes that is a smaller set than the standard grouping, SHIFT-click on all the brushes you want in your set.

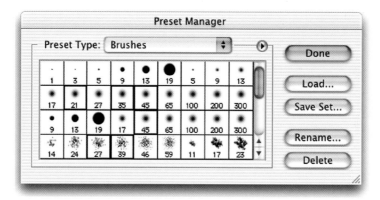

Then click Save Set and, in the dialog box, name your set and determine the location where you'd like to save them.

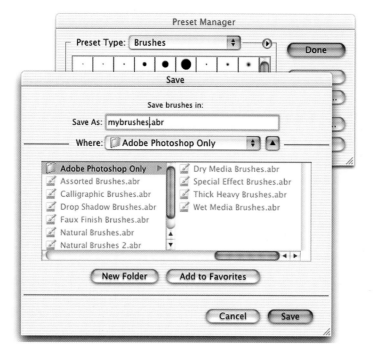

Making your own preset tools

Photoshop 7 offers you the chance to create specific presets for all the tools you use most frequently. Taking advantage of this can really speed up your work. For example, if you use a one-pixel hard brush frequently for painting or retouching, create a preset for it, and it's now ready for you to pick up at any time.

1. Type the letter B to choose the Brush tool.

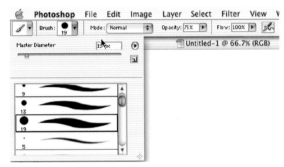

2. Using the Brush Options, make your brush just as you would like it. For example, you might use a one-pixel brush with no dynamics and 1% spacing. Also set the opacity and flow as you want them.

3. If you use one color frequently, choose that too, in your Color Picker.

4. Test your brush on your canvas, to be sure that it looks how you want it.

5. Click the arrow next to the brush picture on the left of the Options bar. This is your **Tool Preset** picker. Once you've opened this you can create new tool presets by clicking on the arrow on the right and selecting **New Tool Preset**.

6. Give your new brush a memorable name, and you're done.

When you create a preset for any tool that uses color, you have the option of including that color. This could be a real timesaver – imagine simply picking a preset that automatically changed the color rather than you having to go to the Color Picker to pick the color yourself! This is very handy for logo work where a certain font and color and size are used as a base for a logo.

Tool Presets can be selected, added and deleted through two locations: the tool icon in the Options bar, or the Tool Presets palette.

Additional presets have been provided and can be loaded for several tools including Type, Brush and Art History. Use the pop-up menu in Tool Presets to see what options are offered.

Reset Tool Presets...
Load Tool Presets...
Save Tool Presets...
Replace Tool Presets...

Art History
Brushes
Crop and Marquee
Text

Remember, you can use the Preset Manager to create your own sub sets of presets that you can load as you need them.

7

Creating custom shapes

Going back to the idea of working with logos – what if you want to have quick access to a vector version of your logo – a version that you can simply drag onto a document? You can do this by adding a custom shape to Photoshop.

1. Activate the Custom Shape tool and take a look at the selection of custom shapes that are available.

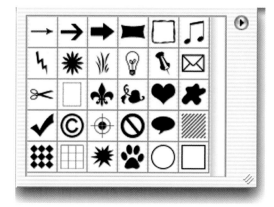

2. Say you want to add an Illustrator logo to these shapes. First, select the logo in Illustrator and copy.

3. Then, switch to Photoshop; create a document (size or resolution doesn't matter) and Paste.

4. You'll get a dialog box asking you whether you want to Paste as Pixels, Path, or Shape Layer. Choose Shape Layer.

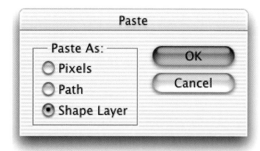

7

5. With the new shape layer active, go to **Edit > Define Custom Shape** and name your shape.

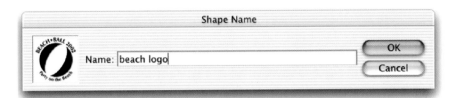

6. To use the new shape, just activate the Custom Shape tool and drag the logo (with the SHIFT key held down to constrain the proportions) as big as you need it.

 You could even create a Tool Preset with the logo shape selected with any pre-chosen color. This avoids having to scroll through the shapes to find your logo and keeps all your favorite options ready to go.

Since shapes are vector, you can make your logo as big as you want and not worry about quality.

Look in the Preset Manager to confirm that your shape is there, and in case you want to create a sub set of shapes as a backup plan.

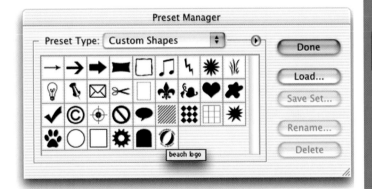

7

When you paste from Illustrator to Photoshop, the graphic may not look the same. This can happen, since some Illustrator functions, such as clipping masks and stroked paths, do not transfer over. To avoid this, use the Illustrator command Expand (from the Object menu) before copying.

If you paste from Illustrator into Photoshop and you do not get the option dialog box to Paste as a Shape Layer, you'll have to change your Preferences in Illustrator. Go to Preferences> Files & Clipboard, you'll have to un-check the PDF option under Clipboard.

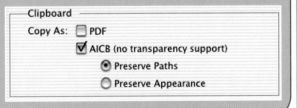

7

Making a custom color palette for accurate color

You can never really trust the color accuracy of your monitor. The colors generated by a monitor and what you reproduce with inks can vary from system to system.

That is why systems such as the **Pantone Color Matching System** (PMS) are such important tools in a designer's arsenal.

You will choose a color from the printed swatch and then choose the color in Photoshop. When you go to print you will know exactly what you are getting.

Here is the default **Swatches** palette:

7

1. Click the small arrow on the top right and choose **PANTONE process coated**, for CMYK (4 color) printing on coated paper. Or **PANTONE solid coated** for spot printing.

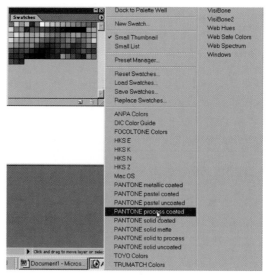

2. A message will pop up asking if you want to replace the current color swatches with these. Click OK to replace the palette with the Pantone palette, or Append to add the colors to the existing color palette.

3. You will now see the Pantone colors. To apply the colors use the eyedropper tool.

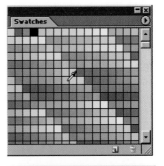

4. Change the display to small list to see the Pantone numbers.

5. Choose the color from the swatch and then find its number in the list to ensure accurate color.

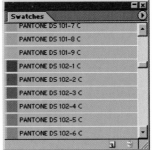

Workspace

Creating custom workspaces

You may want certain palette combinations showing for different situations. For example, I like to have only my Layers palette showing when I have a complex layer document open.

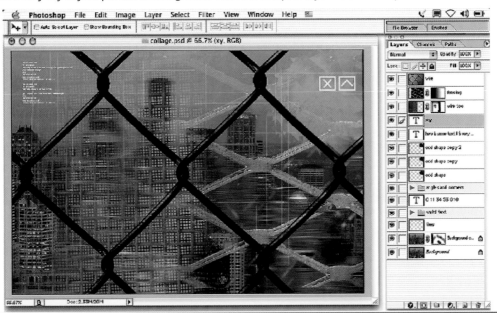

You can save your own custom workspaces and switch between them very quickly, through the **Window > Workspace** command. Here's how:

1. Move all palettes into the position you want. This could include hiding certain palettes or changing their location.

2. From the Window menu, choose **Workspace > Save Workspace**

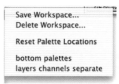

3. Name the custom workspace.

4. Now if you go to **Window > Workspace**, you'll see your new setting from the bottom of the menu.

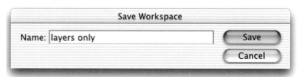

5. To put all palettes back to the default setting, from the Window menu, choose **Workspace > Reset Palette Locations**.

Using the Palette Well

The **Palette Well** is used to store and access palettes, as long as your monitor is large enough. In theory, according to Adobe, if your monitor is at least 800 x 600, you can use the Palette Well. In practice, however, I've worked on a few 800 x 600 monitors where the Well is not visible.

Any palette docked in the Well is considered hidden, so will not have a check mark beside it when you look under the Window menu.

1. To add a palette to the Well, either click on the palette name tab and drag it into the Well, or use a palette's popup menu to choose Dock to Palette Well.

2. To use a palette in the Well, click once on the palette tab.

3. To remove a palette from the Well, click on the palette tab and drag it out of the Well.

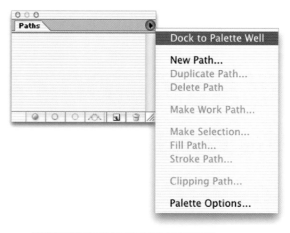

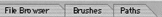

7

Changing units and measurements

When you are viewing an image it's really easy to change the units of measurement.

If the rulers are not visible, press CTRL/CMD+R to show them.

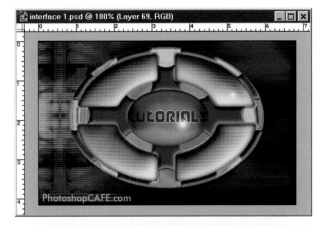

Right/CTRL-click on the rules and a drop-down will appear showing all the options.

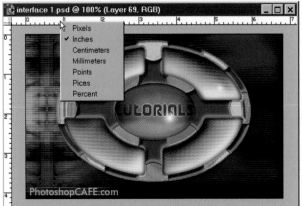

Choose another option and the units will change on the rulers.

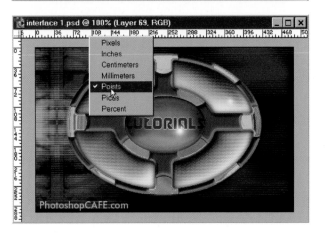

The Preferences window

Many of the changes you can make to the way Photoshop operates are held in the Preferences window, so for this section of the chapter we'll take a walk through some of the most useful options available here, which you can use to increase the speed and efficiency of Photoshop.

Two important notes about preferences:

- Any changes you make will remain as your new default settings until you alter them.

- Change your preferences as often as you need to be more productive - there's no rule that says you can only change your settings once a day.

General Preferences

Open the **Preferences** dialog by pressing CTRL/CMD+K, or look under the Edit menu (Windows and Mac OS System 9) or the Photoshop menu (Windows XP and Mac OS X).

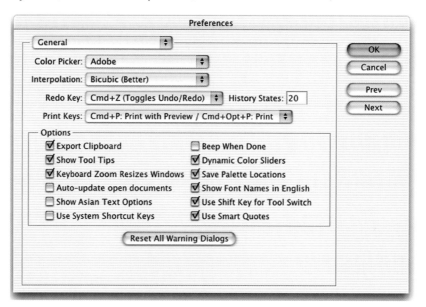

Interpolation

The default for this is **Bicubic**, so leave it like this unless instructed otherwise (by a service provider or perhaps a book) for a specific reason. **Nearest Neighbor** works faster but with less precision and is best reserved for non anti-aliased artwork. Use with caution as it can result in jagged edges. **Bilinear** is the medium quality setting, but realistically, since we want the best quality, we use Bicubic as it is the slowest, but most precise method of interpolation.

History States

This refers to the number of states remembered in the History palette. The default is 20. If you have plenty of RAM, you could change this to a higher number, but it doesn't take much to put a strain on your RAM. You may want to keep this at 20, and increase (or decrease) this number depending on the project you're working on, and the RAM you have available.

Export Clipboard

This option is on by default, allowing pixels you've copied to be pasted in other applications. Again, a personal choice, but in general, copying is not the best way to get images from Photoshop to other software. Typically, it's best to save in some appropriate format and then place or import into the other program. So, if you leave this option checked, it means that you'll encounter a slight delay each time you leave Photoshop, while the Clipboard is exported. Personally, I turned this option off just to save that slight delay.

Use Shift Key for Tool Switch

If you're a seasoned Photoshop user, you'll know that a few versions ago it was easy to switch between the Lasso tools (or any tool with multiple choices such as the Marquee or Stamp tools). You would simply press the same letter repeatedly to switch between tools. Then Adobe decided to add the SHIFT key to the shortcut, making the command to switch Lasso tools L SHIFT L. Now the choice is yours: by default the SHIFT key is on, but you can choose to turn this option off.

File Handling

7

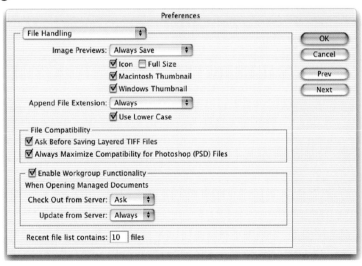

7

Image Previews

In this case the default setting is to include thumbnails when the document is saved. Web designers may choose to turn this off as the thumbnail does add a small amount to the file size – in web design, every K counts. You can choose to **Always Save** thumbnails, **Never Save** thumbnails or **Ask When Saving.** If you want to decide about thumbnails on the fly, choose Ask When Saving and you'll get thumbnail options at the bottom of the dialog box.

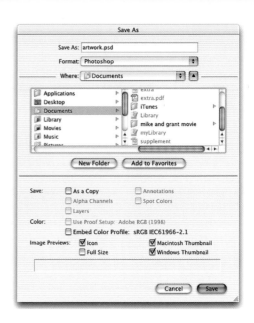

Windows users will notice that they are not offered the extended Thumbnails options, so your dialog box will differ slightly tho the one shown.

Ask Before Saving Layered TIFF Files

Although it is now possible to save a TIFF file that includes layers, be careful here! There are a limited number of applications (other than Photoshop) that support layered TIFF files. This means that if you save a layered document as a TIFF and attempt to place it into a page layout software, it may not work. Leave this checked to ensure that you will get a warning about layered TIFFS (otherwise you could save a layered TIFF and not even realize it).

Always Maximize Compatibility

This preference improves the chance of your Photoshop 7 files being readable in previous versions of Photoshop. There will still be some features that are not supported in earlier versions, such as some blend modes and layer styles. Choosing this option will also mean that a composite (flattened) version is included in the layered document. This composite image is used by other applications when importing a PSD document. If you are dealing with very large files, you may consider turning off this option, but be aware of the drawbacks of doing so. If you save a document as a PSD file with this option turned off, you may encounter problems if you then try to place the file into another program, such as older versions of Illustrator or PageMaker, as these programs are likely to need the composite image. You'll get a message that looks like this:

This layered Photoshop file was not saved with a composite image.

Dieses uberlagerte Photoshop Datei war mit keinem zusammengesezt Bild gespeichert.

この Photoshop ファイルには レイヤーが含まれていますが、 合成画像が保存されていません。

Ce fichier Photoshop multicalques n'a pas été enregistrer avec une image composite

To fix this, you'd have to return to the Preferences, turn on the maximize compatibility, and re-save the file.

Enable Workgroup Functionality

If you are able to connect to a **WebDAV** server then you may wish to use Photoshop's workgroup management features. **WebDAV** or **Web-based Distributed Authoring and Versioning** allows users to collaborate on projects by editing files on remote servers. Photoshop 6 had some WebDAV support, but in the latest version this has been greatly improved.

By using a WebDAV server, a group of designers can work remotely on the same project. As well as being able to download and upload files onto remote servers, it is possible to add your own files, and most importantly to lock a file whilst work is in progress, to ensure that your amends are not lost if the file is accidentally overwritten by another user. To find out more about WebDAV servers go to www.webdav.org.

So, if you are able to connect to a WebDAV server, then check the **Enable Workgroup Functionality** box, and this will bring up the Workgroup pop up menu at the bottom of your screen. If you are not connected to a WebDAV server, then checking this option will have no affect.

Check out from server: You can choose three options when checking a file out from a server:

- **Never:** You will never be able to open a file locally, which has not been checked out

- **Always:** Will automatically check out the file when you open it

- **Ask:** Will display a dialog box, before you can open a file that has not been checked out

Update from Server: There are three similar options when updating a file.

- **Never:** Means that you will not be able to open the file, without first downloading the latest version from the server

- **Always:** Will automatically download the latest updates from the server

- **Ask:** Means that when you open the file, you'll be asked if you wish to download the latest version from the server

Recent file list

Although the default setting is to remember the last 10 files you've opened, Photoshop actually remembers the last 30 files, so why not change this setting to 30, have quick access to more of your recent files, and save having to search through piles of files and folders to get to the work you're looking for.

Display & Cursors

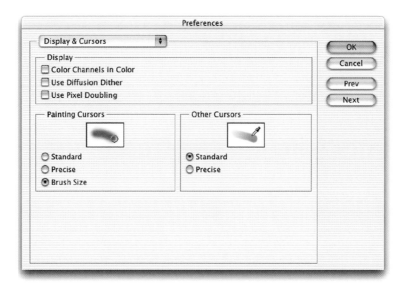

It is best to keep the Painting Cursor set to Brush Size, as this helps you to gauge the size of your brush strokes when painting. If you ever need to use the Precise cursor just turn on CAPS LOCK and the Brush Cursor will change to the Precise cursor. Same theory with the Other Cursors: I'd leave this set at Standard and use the CAPS LOCK key if you need the Precise cursor.

Transparency & Gamut

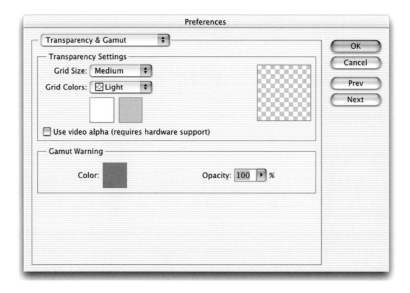

7

There are two types of Photoshop user... those who find it helpful to have transparency indicated by the transparency checkerboard, and those who run to turn this off as quickly as possible.

Personally, I wasn't a big fan, especially when I ended up with white objects on a transparent layer – very difficult to see.

In the Preferences dialog you can now choose a light, medium, or dark gray background, or a pre-set color background. You can also customize your own background, by clicking on the color squares and changing them to pink and darker gray.

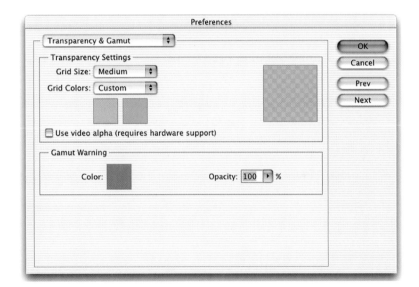

With this background, white objects are very easy to see.

Naturally, if you often work with pink objects, then you can choose an alternative contrasting color.

Here is some small white text on the transparency checkerboard, with some white paint underneath

Units & Rulers

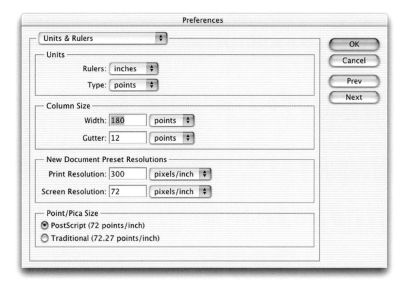

Column Size

This option works wonders when you are using Photoshop in conjunction with page layout software. You set up your document in XPress or InDesign and make a note of the column width you've created, and the size of the gutter. Enter those values in this preference dialogue box

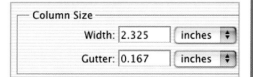

From now on, if you want to create Photoshop documents that will fit to the exact width of 2 columns, you can use columns as a unit of measurement, and Photoshop will do the math for you (1 column + gutter + 1 column).

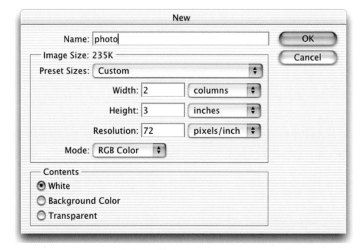

Or, to change an existing image, use the same concept by changing the measurement in the Image Size dialog to columns.

Just change the settings when you change your page layout file.

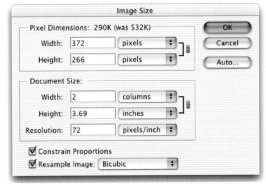

New Document Preset Resolutions
To understand the value of this option we need a little background. Photoshop 7 allows you to create your own preset sizes for new documents, so that you can quickly and easily create new documents of specific sizes. Let's briefly look at this now.

Making your own custom sizes
When you're creating your own custom document sizes you need to specify the proportions in a text file.

Look in the main Photoshop folder for a folder called Presets, and in that folder you'll see a file called New Doc Size.txt. Open this file with any text editor and follow the instructions in the file to add your own sizes.

As you can see resolution is defined as either print or screen, or an actual numeric value. But what resolution does either print or screen relate to? This is where the **New Document Preset Resolutions** option comes into play. This is where you can set the default screen and print resolution.

The beauty of this option is that you could create several different document sizes that all use print as their resolution. Then, if you decide you need to change all of these from 300 to 266 ppi. It's easy to do that by simply going to the Preferences dialog.

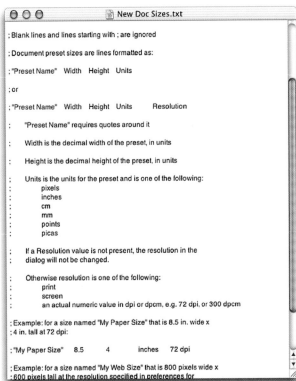

7

To take advantage of the resolution preference, just add either screen or print to the description of your file. Once you've added to the text file and re-saved, the new size will appear in the **File > New** dialog box.

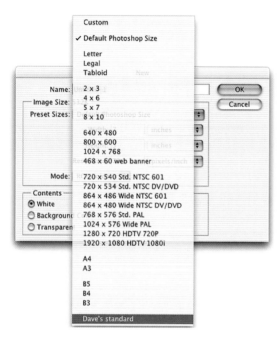

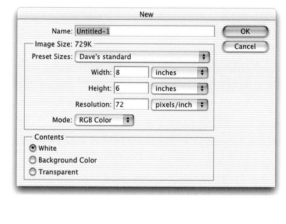

Guides, Grid & Slices

This set of preferences is almost entirely down to personal taste. Here you can select the color of guides and the appearance of grids and slices to your own taste and work methods.

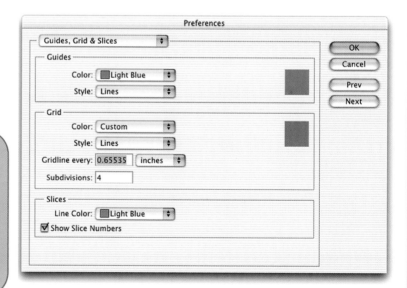

If you're working on a document and want to change the color of the guides, just hold down CTRL/CMD and double-click on a guide to get directly to this dialog box so you can change the settings, such as color.

7

Plug-ins & Scratch Disks

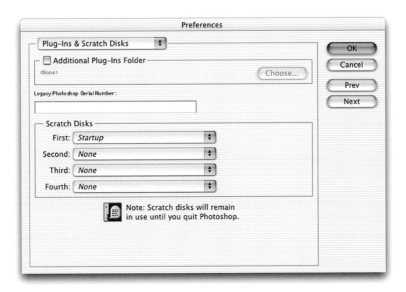

Additional Plug-ins folder

Here you can choose whether you want an additional plug-in folder and the option to add a serial number to get older plug-ins to work. The theory behind indicating an additional plug-in folder is to cut down on the size of your Filter menu. You could move infrequently used filters into another folder, to be loaded only when required. The only downside is that you must restart Photoshop when you want to add these extra filters.

To load the plug-in folders either change the preference to indicate the location of the additional plug-in folder, or hold down CTRL/CMD+SHIFT as you restart Photoshop. With this keyboard command, Photoshop will pause as it reloads, asking you to choose an additional plug-in folder.

If you have an older plug-in that doesn't work in Photoshop 7, you can try entering your serial number from Photoshop 6 or earlier in the legacy serial number box. It still may not work, but it just might!

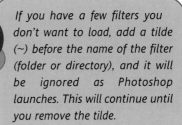

If you have a few filters you don't want to load, add a tilde (~) before the name of the filter (folder or directory), and it will be ignored as Photoshop launches. This will continue until you remove the tilde.

7

Scratch Disks

Have you ever been plagued by those **Scratch Disk is Full** messages? The solution to this is to increase your scratch disk space through this dialogue box setting. By default, your start-up disk is the first, or primary, disk that Photoshop uses as virtual memory. If you have more than one hard drive or a partitioned disk, you can tell Photoshop which disks to use. Ideally, choose a large, empty drive or partition as your first scratch disk, and your start-up disk as your second. It is not recommended to use network drives or removable storage as scratch disks.

Memory & Image Cache

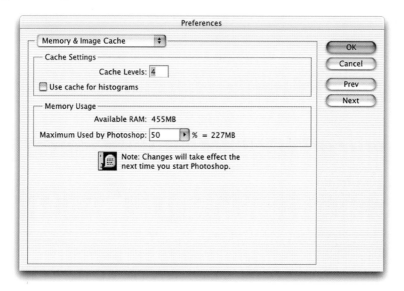

Cache is used for screen re-draw and histogram display. 1 is the minimum and 8 is the maximum, so 4 is a good medium setting to balance speed and accuracy. In general, unless specifically advised to do so by an expert, it is best to leave the Cache Levels at this default.

Leave **Use cache for histograms** unchecked - when it is checked the display of the histogram (in dialog boxes such as Levels) is faster, but less accurate. As for amount of RAM allocated to Photoshop, give as much as you can afford – 50% is common, but be aware that this could leave you unable to run several applications at once.

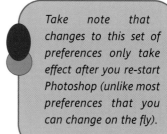

Take note that changes to this set of preferences only take effect after you re-start Photoshop (unlike most preferences that you can change on the fly).

Resetting preferences

Sometimes the Preferences file becomes corrupted for whatever reason, and this basically means that it is giving poor or wrong instructions to Photoshop. Examples of this would be things such as, you enter 100% yellow in the Color Picker, and it displays more like green. Or, standard shortcuts suddenly don't work, menus are displaying improperly, or other strange and unexplainable things are happening.

When this happens sometimes the best remedy is to simply delete your preferences. This will let you create a brand new, fresh set of preferences. To delete your preferences you need to find the file called `Adobe Photoshop 7.0 Prefs.psp` and delete it.

Here's where you find the Preferences file, depending on your platform and operating system:

- **Mac OSX**: User (username) > Library > Preferences > Adobe Photoshop7.0 Settings > Adobe Photoshop7.0 Prefs

- **Mac OS 9**: System Folder > Preferences > Adobe Photoshop 7 Settings > Adobe Photoshop 7 Prefs

- **Windows**: Documents and Settings > (username) > Application Data > Adobe > Photoshop 7.0> Adobe Photoshop7.0 Settings > Adobe Photoshop7.0 Prefs

Alternatively, if you click CTRL/CMD+ALT+SHIFT as you launch Photoshop, you'll see the following message pop up:

Click OK and a new Preferences file will be created with the original factory defaults restored.

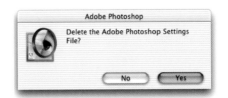

7

Remember that deleting preferences will change all settings, so any that you had previously set will be gone. So here's another approach: once you have all your personal settings established, make a copy of the Preferences file and store it safely away. Then if your preferences start acting up, replace the bad Preferences file with the good one you stored away.

Other settings

There are a number of Photoshop settings that aren't part of the Preferences, but can be changed as kind of a global setting. It's easy to tell what you can (and cannot) change as one of these overall settings: launch Photoshop but don't open a document. Then take a look to see which menus are available (not grayed out). Look under those menus to see which options are available. Anything you can change is, in effect, a default setting.

For example, many layer styles use Global Light to determine the look of the effect. Rather than changing the setting every time you use a layer style, change the default setting using this method. With no documents open, look under the Layer menu and you'll see that only Layer Styles is available. Under that menu, only Global Light is an option.

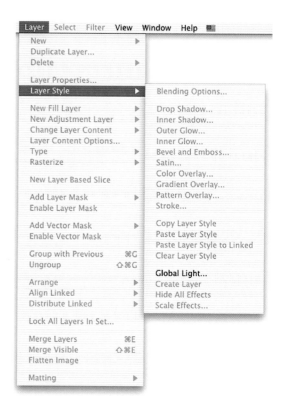

Change the setting and that will be your default setting for global light.

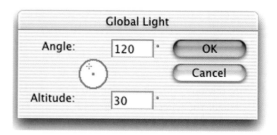

7

The same concept can be applied to other settings, such as **Proof Colors**. Under the View menu is a command called Proof Colors (CTRL/CMD+Y). This command lets you preview how a document will look in another mode – by default the mode is CMYK. If you always want a different mode and don't want to repeatedly visit the View menu and Proof Setup, use our default method by going to the View menu with no documents open and choosing your proof choice.

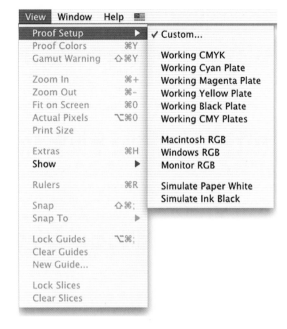

On-line preferences

Adobe maintains a series of areas for Photoshop users, containing tutorial, common problems and program updates. To access these easily, just click on the graphic at the very top of the toolbox. You can also set it up so Photoshop will check for you to look for updates and other information that can help you. To do this, click on the graphic to open the Adobe Online dialog box, then click the Preferences button. You can now decide how often (if at all) you want to automatically check for updates. Clearly for all of these features you need to have an active internet connection.

Color Settings

The Color Settings dialog box enables you to create color management systems. You can access it by going to **Edit > Color Settings** (Windows) and **Photoshop > Color Settings** (Mac), or use the shortcut CTRL/CMD+SHIFT+K There are varying opinions on color management systems: whether or not to use them, what settings to use, and how much to rely on them, are just some of the questions often asked. You'll need to discuss with your print shop or service bureau the implications of using a color management system. There are however, a couple of key settings you should look at regardless of your ultimate decision.

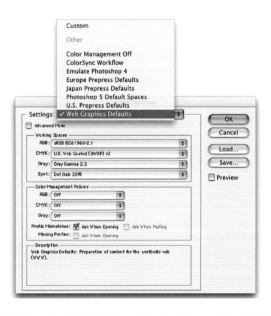

7

In the Settings field, you'll probably find that Web Graphics Defaults is on by default. As the name suggests, this setting is intended for web design, so if you're doing print work, then this may not be an appropriate choice, and you need to consider changing it. If you're preparing for print and have not received specific advice from a print shop, choose one of the prepress settings such as **U.S. Prepress Defaults.**

Here's a neat trick to make sure you are never tempted to pick a color out of the CMYK gamut. Open the Color Picker and then from the View menu choose Gamut Warning, or press CTRL/CMD+SHIFT+Y. *Now all colors that are out of the CMYK gamut will be shown with a gray overlay.*

The most important thing to remember here is to get some advice from your service bureau or print shop.

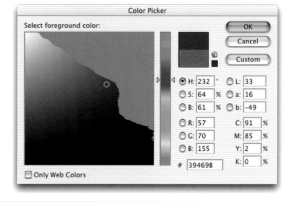

7

Using Actions to set up keyboard shortcuts for anything

There are a lot of commands that do not have a preset shortcut to them. For example, I wish I had a dollar for every time I have heard someone ask about a shortcut to crop an image. Yes I know the C key will active the Crop tool, but that doesn't apply the tool to the image.

There is a way you can apply a shortcut to everything, by using actions and assigning a shortcut to the action.

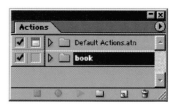

1. Go to the **Actions** palette, and click the **Create new set** button. This is where we will save all our command set actions.

2. To create a new action, click the New Action button and name it crop tool.

3. Now for the shortcut key: Choose a **Function Key** and add a modifier. You can also give the action a color to separate it from the other actions. This will display it in the chosen color in the palette.

4. Click Record.

5. You are now on the air, and whatever you do will be recorded into the action. Select the Crop tool and drag out a crop in the image area.

6. Right/CTRL-click and choose Apply, or just double-click in the crop area to apply the crop.

7. Press the Stop button to stop recording the action.

7

7

8. Click the expander arrows to see the contents of the action.

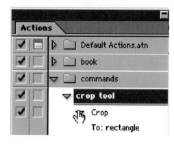

9. If you were to run the action now, it would crop all the images exactly the same size as the example, starting from the same XY co-ordinates. Plus, if you have an image that is smaller than the recorded action's cropped area, the smaller image will resize itself to that cropped size, leaving a large background-colored canvas area surrounding the original picture. So we will insert a dialog option step.

10. Click the first checkbox next to the action and the box will show a dialog icon.

11. To test the action open an image and press the Play button.

12. The Crop tool will now appear waiting for you to resize and apply it.

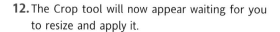

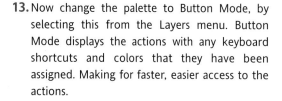

13. Now change the palette to Button Mode, by selecting this from the Layers menu. Button Mode displays the actions with any keyboard shortcuts and colors that they have been assigned. Making for faster, easier access to the actions.

Here is our Actions palette in Button Mode. Note our action is shown with the color we assigned to it. It also displays the shortcut CTRL/CMD+ F2.

14. Let's test it. Open an image.

15. Press CTRL+F2 and adjust your crop area by dragging on the handles.

16. Apply the crop and we have cropped the image in one-step!

The shortcut will also work in regular mode in the Actions palette – it's just easier to see it in button mode. Use this technique to save time with all your commonly used tasks. You can also automate multiple steps in one action. For example, when processing images for a magazine, I will create an action that will crop, set levels, set color balance, sharpen and convert to CMYK mode.

7

RAM

Software settings for hardware

Display adapter

Monitor

Mouse

Graphics tablets

Processor

Peripherals

Customizing your workspace

8: Hardware options

Photoshop is a pretty intense program, making high demands on your system resources. Setting up your hardware correctly can mean the difference between crawling and flying. Let's take a look at some common hardware queries, and look at the ways in which your hardware options can help you get the best out of Photoshop.

RAM

RAM is short for **random access memory**; this is the type of memory used by your computer to run your operating system, applications, and any other data in current use. Information is stored temporarily using RAM, whilst your hard drive and other storage devices retain data permanently.

RAM is akin to short-term memory – quick and easy to access, but only capable of holding a limited number of items. Experts reckon that the average human being can hold seven pieces of information in their short-term memory at one time. If you think of seven things and then try to hold onto an eighth thought, inevitably something will pop out of your head. With your computer, this happens when you try to run applications that use more RAM than you have available. Photoshop is notorious for eating up RAM and the result is frequent crashes, or lots of painful waiting around whilst your images are rendered. We'll look at ways to avoid this frustration, and consider whether or not you need to acquire more RAM.

We measure RAM in the same way we measure hard drive space: using bytes (which is a basic computer unit of information), kilobytes (1,024 bytes), megabytes (1,024 kilobytes), and even gigabytes (1,024 megabytes).

RAM comes in multiples of 8 megabytes (Mb), and is sold bundled into sets of 16Mb. The minimum recommendation is 32Mb, most modern computers have 128Mb of RAM increasing to 256, 512 and beyond. But just how much do you need?

How much RAM do I need to run Photoshop?

The amount of RAM you need depends upon how you intend to use Photoshop, but also remember that Photoshop *itself* takes a good amount of RAM to run. As a basic rule, you should have three times more RAM than the file you're trying to open. So if your file is 10Mb, you'll need 30Mb of RAM *on top of* your other memory requirements. Remember that your operating system will need some of your RAM memory to run; as does every application you have open, including Photoshop itself. So, to open a 10Mb file you're probably going to need at least 64Mb of RAM. 32Mb in this case would be cutting it a bit fine.

The price of RAM fluctuates, sometimes it can be expensive to buy, but it is generally possible to buy cheap RAM online, in some cases you can get as much as 256 Mb for as little as 50 USD, this will significantly increase your machine's speed at relatively low cost.

Web versus print

In general, print work will require more RAM than web graphics, due to larger file sizes. Images destined for print need a resolution of at least 300ppi to ensure a good quality print, (at the risk of stating the obvious this results in a larger image size in terms of the number of pixels). For the web, you only need a resolution of 72dpi – less than a third of the size you need for print; an A5 size image at 72dpi is around 976Kb, whilst at 300dpi the same file size is 16.5Mb.

Photoshop will need more memory to remember the file. If you don't have enough RAM and Photoshop can't load the entire file into memory in one go it will load a part of it to your scratch disk, before loading the next part of the file. Obviously this means things are going to go a lot slower – as lots of swapping has to take place.

So, if you're going to be working in print, you should have between 512Mb and 1Gb of RAM to ensure that Photoshop operates smoothly.

This does not mean, however, that working for the web only requires a third of the RAM. The more layers and effects you add in Photoshop, the larger your file size will be. You'll be surprised how fast this can get out of hand! While we don't need quite as much RAM for web work as for print work, we still need at least 256Mb to be safe, particularly if you want to use other RAM-hungry programs such as Dreamweaver at the same time. The ideal amount of RAM would be 512Mb.

We've all noticed that, as operating systems become more advanced, they require more RAM (they get greedy!). The same goes for Photoshop. So plan to upgrade your RAM about once every two years. On the Mac, using OS9, Photoshop runs better with virtual memory on (using the hard drive as RAM), which can save on the amount of actual RAM you need, but there isn't a real substitute for extra memory.

You do also get different speeds of RAM (measured in nanoseconds), but this isn't as important as some computer salespeople would have you believe. Getting more RAM is better than getting faster RAM.

> *Remember that you don't have to have more RAM, if you're prepared to go and make coffee every time Photoshop renders the image...*

How do I make the most out of how Photoshop uses my RAM?

We will see later on in the chapter how to use the hard drive as a replacement for not having enough RAM (using scratch disks), but regardless of how much RAM you have, it's a good idea to make a decision on how much you should let Photoshop use.

On Windows and Mac OSX, Photoshop will use half of your available RAM by default. In Mac OS9 and earlier, you need to set this level manually by going to **Photoshop > Get Info**.

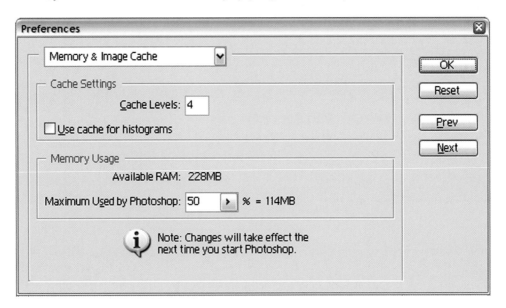

In the above image, the computer in question has 256Mb of RAM. As you can see, Windows requires 28Mb of RAM to run, which leaves us with 228Mb available.

So how much RAM do we give Photoshop to play with?

Ideally, you should close other programs while using Photoshop, then you'd be free to allocate as much as 60% or 70% of your available RAM to it. Unfortunately, in the real world we often need to run other memory intensive software at the same time as Photoshop. Assigning a huge chunk of your RAM to Photoshop will mean severely degrading the performance of your other programs. The key here, is to prioritize the programs you'll be using, and decide which one requires better performance.

If you have too many programs using too much of the available RAM then a lot of memory will have to be written to scratch disk, which is going to slow the entire process down.

Software settings for hardware

We mentioned earlier that if you don't have enough RAM, your system will use a swapping system with your hard drive and remember as much as it can at a time. Using your hard drive like this is called creating a 'scratch disk'.

How do I set up a scratch disk?

In Windows you need to go to **Edit > Preferences > Plug-ins & Scratch Disks**, in Mac OSX the Preferences are found under the Photoshop menu.

Select the hard drives that you want to use as scratch disks from the drop-down box. It's as easy as that. As you can see from the above image, I only have one hard drive present, so the scratch disk has been set to the startup volume – my local hard drive.

Ok, so what's the best way to use a scratch disk?

If you want to get the best performance out of your scratch disk(s), here are some tips:

- Try to have your scratch disk on a different hard drive to the files you're editing, especially if you're dealing with large file sizes. The less congestion you have between loading and saving files and using your scratch disks the better.

- If you already use a hard drive for virtual memory, where possible use a different hard drive for your scratch disk. Only one piece of information can be written to a particular drive at a time. If you're using different drives, more information can be written at the same time, this is true even if you have partitioned the drive.

- Make sure your scratch disks are local drives. It is a very bad idea to use a network drive as your scratch disk: not only will it be very slow, but you also risk untimely disconnections, and difficulties in gaining access, no matter how big the network drive.

- Don't use a removable drive as your scratch disk, specifically if you're able to remove it while your computer is still running (hot swappable). Photoshop will have issues with you when it dumps memory to this drive and then you promptly remove it. Big issues.

- Because of the nature of the way scratch disks work, even though Photoshop removes the information when you close it down, it's a good idea to defragment these drives on a regular basis. (This is another good reason to avoid networks, as remote stations are seldom permitted to do remote utilities on networks). This will increase the longevity of the hard drive, but more importantly speed up the drive access and therefore speed up Photoshop.

8

Increasing the resolution of your monitor

We've already mentioned resolution. If you only have one monitor available to you and you can't afford a larger monitor, one way to avoid wading through a sea of palettes is to increase the resolution. This will make all the palettes a lot smaller and give you back some of that precious space you need for your image.

The downside to this is that increasing the resolution of the monitor places additional strain on both your display adapter, as it's now got to send far more information to the monitor (there are suddenly far more pixels after all), *and* your monitor (it's suddenly got to display a lot more). Depending on how good your monitor is, you might find that it isn't able to refresh the screen fast enough, and you'll be bumped back down to a bad refresh rate (less than 75Hz). If this is the case, it's better to use the TAB key to hide/display all the palettes than place undue strain on your eyes.

You can also increase the color depth that your computer uses. This is the range of colors in use. The more colors you use, the smoother and richer your resultant images will be.

Unfortunately, using more color means placing similar additional strain on your hardware as mentioned above. There is an additional concern as well: most people don't run in really high color modes. If you're doing web work, chances are most people will view your images quite differently to the way you created them.

Display adapter

This piece of hardware, also known as a graphics adapter, display card or sometimes (incorrectly) as a video card, is responsible for interpreting the stuff that goes on inside your computer into images that can be displayed on your monitor/screen. These cards also have memory (RAM) on them which is used to determine how much can be sent to the screen before the card has to go get more information. Fetching more information obviously takes time, so as usual, the more RAM you have on the card, the better.

- Traditionally, Macs are more geared towards graphics than PCs are. This means that when you buy a Mac, the display adapter that comes with it is usually of a high enough quality not to need to change it.

- With PCs however, there's a fairly good chance that it will have an inferior display adapter. The up side is you have more control over *what* you buy. For example, if you're serious about using Photoshop, you can go out and get a display adapter that's specifically designed for Photoshop. Most of the discussion that follows regarding display adapters is for PC users.

What's the best display adapter to use for Photoshop?

Strangely enough, the best display cards that are coming out these days are often not the best cards to get for Photoshop. Most display adapters on the market today cater to high-end 3D games. Different parts of the card are used for different things. One part of the card will be used to render 3D graphics, while another part of it will deal with 2D. Also, as I mentioned before, graphics cards depend on their own RAM.

8

What we need for Photoshop is a display adapter with good 2D rendering. No matter how fast the card is at playing games, this will be useless to us unless the card is also capable of excellent 2D rendering speeds.

Because there are so many display adapters on the market, it's impossible to recommend a specific one. When choosing a display adapter that's good for Photoshop, keep two things in mind:

- Firstly, not all RAM is created equal. This is especially true of RAM on display adapters. Some people are able to think faster than others – this is also true of computer components. What we are looking for here is a display adapter with a large forehead and a string of astrophysics degrees. For our purposes, we want a display card that has **DDR RAM** (**double data rate RAM**) – a really fast kind of RAM.

- Secondly, don't fall for cards advertising, "Blazing 3D Speeds," because this is fairly irrelevant to us. Great if you're running 3D Studio Max, pointless if you're running Photoshop. If you have access to the web, check out www.tomshardware.com, which offers comparisons of different hardware speeds.

Most graphics cards these days are **AGP** (**Accelerated Graphics Port)** compatible. All the latest computers have a special slot designed specifically for graphics cards that you can plug them into. These cards are generally much faster than the standard **PCI** (**Peripheral Component Interconnect**) graphics cards. So if your motherboard has an AGP slot in it, these cards are the ones to get.

One final point on this matter: get a display adapter with more than 16Mb of RAM. With display adapters you can really see the difference as far as RAM is concerned.

8

Monitor

With some Macs, changing the monitor isn't an option – the entire computer is built into it! For those not in possession of a pretty iMac, however, you generally have the option of replacing the monitor, so we'll look at the factors involved when choosing a monitor.

What size monitor should I get?

In the world of computer graphics, when it comes to monitors it's simply a question of the bigger, the better. Right now, the best value for money seems to be a 17-inch monitor, although if you shop around you should be able to find a 19-inch monitor for less than 300 USD. It's worth checking out some technology web sites such as www.cnet.com to find some good deals. Anything bigger gets alarmingly expensive, and anything smaller will make working with large images very frustrating.

Something to take into account is: the bigger your monitor and the higher the resolution (number of pixels on the screen), the greater the demand on your display adapter. This is hardly noticeable with smaller screens, but when you get to a 21-inch monitor there can be a fairly significant impact on performance. The best advice here is to be sure to have the **appropriate graphics card for your monitor**.

What type of monitor should I get?

The most important issue here is, not the make of the monitor, but the **Dot Pitch**, which refers to the size of the pixels. The smaller the pixels (which is obviously also something that's governed by the resolution you're in) the smoother your image will appear. A standard dot pitch is around 0.28, 0.26 is a very good dot pitch.

Resolution is also a point for discussion. Most monitors these days can easily offer a resolution of 1024x768 pixels, which represents the number of pixels fitted onto the screen's length and height.

A lot of designers like to run in really high resolutions, as much as 1600x1200, but remember that if you're designing for the web, most people don't run in such high resolution, with the majority still somewhere around 800x600. If you've created an image in 1600x1200 it will be pretty much double the size on a screen running in 800x600 resolution. Also, any little specks or flaws in your design will suddenly be a lot larger!

When designing for the web, it's important to test your design at varying resolutions to see what it will look like to other people.

8

Should I do anything to the monitor besides unpacking it?

Monitors usually also require calibration. It is well known that different screens display color differently, which is a bit of a headache for print and web designers alike. For print designers, you'd like to know that what you're designing on the screen is going to look the same way on paper. The same goes for a web designer: you want your graphics to look the same on everyone's screens. Therefore, an important part of the process of designing in Photoshop is to calibrate the color, brightness, and contrast of the monitor.

Most monitors these days ship with **ICC** (**International Color Consortium**) profiles, which means you can get your monitor to display color accurately across platforms. This works in the following way: color is displayed on your computer screen using a system of numbers. These numbers represent percentages of color – expressed in the amount of red, green, and blue each pixel should be. Combining equal amounts of red, green, and blue light together gives you white light. We can express almost any color in terms of percentages of these three.

What an ICC color profile will do is adjust the intensity of each of these colors based on a built-in system that knows how your monitor displays color. For example, all monitors of brand X display color with a slightly reddish tint and monitors of brand Y a slightly greenish tint. If both have ICC profiles, when you open an image in Photoshop and choose to use an embedded color profile, if your monitor is brand X the profile will display the color taking the reddish tint into account. If you have a brand Y monitor, the image will be displayed with less green and more red and blue so that it appears the same.

When buying a monitor, try to get the ICC profile that comes with it. If you don't have your monitor's ICC profile, you could try search online for the information. Once you have an ICC profile that you can use go to **Image > Mode > Assign Profile** to embed your ICC color profile (at the slight sacrifice of file size) to ensure consistency of color when displaying an image on multiple platforms.

A good place to start with calibration of your monitor is to use the **Adobe Gamma** tool, which ships with Photoshop, and lives in your Control Panel directory. Adobe Gamma will help you calibrate your monitor to get the most out of color, brightness and contrast. This can make a huge difference to the work you produce with Photoshop, especially when you want to send it to someone else, or view someone else's work.

One last thing to set up to get the most out of your monitor is the **refresh rate**. The refresh rate is the speed at which your monitor can update the entire screen. Your monitor has to completely redraw the screen many times a second. Responsibility for this task is shared between your display adapter and your monitor.

The display adapter and the monitor work together. Your display adapter sends the information to your monitor, and your monitor tries its best to display it. If one is capable of greater speed than the other, you will still only be able to run at the lower rate.

The slower the refresh rate, the more flicker produced by your screen. You may have noticed this on televisions, which often have fairly low refresh rates. This isn't really a problem, as you're not likely to sit right up close to a TV. With a monitor it's a different story. You may be working on Photoshop for hours at a stretch; if the screen is flickering constantly then you risk damaging your eyes. On some operating systems the default refresh rate is as low as 60Hz – if possible you should change this.

8

If you're in Windows, what you need to do is to right-click your Desktop, go to **Properties > Settings** and click on the **Advanced** button, to get a new set of options tabs. Go to **Monitor** and under **Monitor settings** you'll see a drop-down box, showing the refresh rates that your monitor is capable of displaying.

Most display adapters are capable of sending information faster than the monitor can actually display it, so beneath this drop-down box is a check box which will allow you to see the refresh rates your card is capable of if it weren't limited by your monitor.

Using a higher refresh rate than your monitor can handle will damage your monitor so don't try it. If you're like me and try out of curiosity, you'll notice it actually makes the flicker worse. The monitor isn't very good at faking it...!

A refresh rate of 75Hz is the bare minimum you should use. I'd recommend at least 85Hz, and if you can get 100Hz out of your monitor, all the better.

For Mac OSX, all you need to do is go to the **System Preferences** icon in your toolbox, and click on **Displays**. For Mac OS9, click on **Monitors and Sound** control panel.

Mouse

Mice come in all shapes and sizes, some with scroll wheels, some using infra red, some with roller-balls some with lasers. All of them can be banged on your desk in frustration when you accidentally close a file without saving it. A good way to relieve stress and a great way to make the person you buy your hardware from rich.

8

What's the best mouse to get if I'm using Photoshop?

Traditional mice use a rubber coated ball and rollers to send signals to your computer. The problem with this is that after a while the rollers get all clogged up with grime which makes the movement of the mouse erratic. This can be particularly irritating when you're doing fine and precise selection work.

A good solution is to get an **optical mouse**.. Instead of using a roller-ball, an optical mouse uses a laser beam to take a tiny low resolution image of your mouse pad. As you move the mouse, the mouse software compares these images and moves your mouse pointer appropriately.

The advantages of using this type of mouse:

- You have far greater control when using your mouse at low speeds. With a traditional rubber-ball kind of mouse there is a minimum speed you can move your mouse at – some speed is needed to overcome the friction between the ball and the rollers. This is not the case with an optical mouse.

- The optical mouse is able to send information to the computer at a much faster rate than most traditional roller-ball mice, again giving you greater control.

- There are no rollers to clean, and no need to clean the mouse as often.

- You actually don't even need a mouse pad: this type of mouse can be used on nearly any surface (except glass and other reflective surfaces), even your duvet!

The disadvantages:

- Occasionally, especially when using the mouse on a surface that has no differences in color at all (so that the mouse can compare the tiny snaps it takes and tell the difference) it loses the plot and jumps around a bit. This is easily overcome by using a mouse-pad with an image on it or any surface with a bit of visual variation in it.

- It's not as much fun to bang it on the desk, as it's quite a bit more expensive to replace.

The Mac mouse can usually be distinguished from the PC mouse by its astonishing lack of a second mouse button. Photoshop reveals many handy built-in functions activated by a right-click. Mac users are stuck using Ctrl-click – which means you have to use both hands (the horror). To combat this nightmare, you could buy an Intellimouse, produced by Microsoft and compatible with Mac OS8.6-9.x and OSX.

> *Make sure that your mouse fits your hand. If the mouse is too small or too big it might be a bit unwieldy, which will affect some of your work that requires fine movements.*

8

Which settings should I adjust to best use my mouse?

Consider adjusting your mouse speed. If you're going to be doing fine adjustment work, it's important not to use a mouse movement setting that's too sensitive. If you're using Windows, there is an icon to change mouse settings in your Control Panel. Roughly half-way should be a slow enough speed to do fine selection work and still prevent you from having to pick the mouse up to avoid driving off the edge of the mouse pad.

For the Mac, go to **System Preferences** and click on **Mouse**. Here you can adjust the tracking speed and double-click speed.

Graphics tablets

One of the most important things to an artist is their brush or pencil. So, why do digital artists endure using a mouse? Drawing with a mouse has been likened to drawing with soap-on-a-rope! Using a pen on a tablet is much more natural, precise, safe, and comfortable for doing graphics and photography work.

"Safe?" Yes! By this I mean that you are much more likely to suffer from repetitive stress injuries, such as Carpal Tunnel Syndrome, if you are using a mouse for this sort of work. Your hand just isn't made to work that way for long stretches of time! With a tablet in your lap, or beside your keyboard, and a good chair, you will cause much less wear on your body.

In addition to this, Photoshop 7 has 19 pressure sensitive tools that can only be accessed with a graphics tablet. Features such as shape dynamics and color dynamics can be affected by the pressure you exert with your pen!

8

The tablet consists of a flat panel, which is corded, and a pen, which is not. The tablet has a clear plastic overlay, which can be lifted and used for tracing. Depending upon its model, you might have programmable buttons across the top with which you can perform particular functions. The pen has a tip end and an eraser end. It also has a rocker switch, which is similarly programmable.

The cordless pen looks and feels just like a regular pen, and you can use it to draw directly on the tablet, which is translated to the screen. As you press harder, the line can get thicker, and the paint darker. As you tilt the pen (new in Photoshop 7) the tip shape will change just like a real piece of chalk or calligraphic pen.

Which tablet to buy?

There are many graphics tablets on the market now, ranging from 49 USD to thousands of dollars, depending on your needs and budget. The market leader is Wacom.

Wacom makes two consumer lines of tablets: the Intuos, which supports 1024 levels of pressure sensitivity and pen tilt, this is well suited for professionals. For less money they have the scaled down Graphire, which only supports 512 levels of sensitivity. That's still 511 more levels than your mouse!

At the Wacom website at www.wacom.com you will find a tablet wizard, which can help you to choose the best tablet in an appropriate size for you. Their advice is based upon how you will be using the tablet, your desk size, size of your strokes, and your monitor size.

Installing a tablet

To install the tablet first open the control panel.

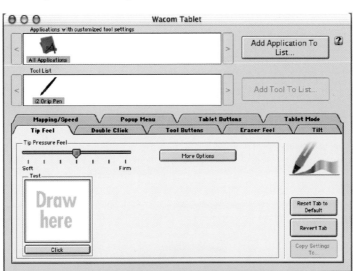

8

You will have to add Photoshop to the list of applications. This will activate all the features in Photoshop.

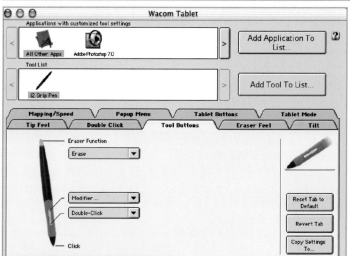

You can set various pen options in this control panel, including programming the buttons on the pen and the button menus on the tablet.

Once you are in Photoshop, open the Brushes properties palette to set your options.

Just choose pen in the drop-down to set the attributes to use the tablet.

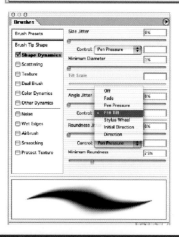

8

Using the Brush Dynamics with your tablet

For both of the following examples, I set the **Brush Tip Shape** to a hard round brush of 30 pixels and spacing of 130%. In the first example, I used the **Shape Dynamics** option set to **Pen Pressure**. For the second example, I used the same settings, but added some **Color Dynamics**.

Each of these examples is just a single brush stroke! Each begins with very light pressure, and increases to firm pressure. For the second one, I let up on the pressure to finish the stroke.

Using a tablet, you can get in very tight and accurately when you are masking, and your stroke remains being a very natural pen stroke.

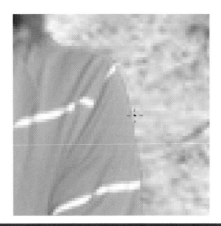

Mastering the tablet

After you have worked (and played) with your tablet for a couple of days, you will have gotten used to the clicking dance. Here's the rundown for this:

- **Single-click:** Tap your pen tip on the tablet.

- **Right-click:** Hold your pen tip right over your tablet and push the forward part of the rocker button. I use my index finger for this forward button.

- **Double-click:** Either tap the pen twice in quick succession (the speed for this can be set in your tablet options in Control Panel), OR click the top of the rocker button on your pen. I use my thumb to push this button. Once you get used to the thumb button, you may find it easier to use than the double-tap.

8

Tablet buttons: *With the Intuos tablets you have a menu strip across the top of the tablet. These buttons are programmable to perform just about any function you want; keystroke combinations, or even typing frequently used text. You can make the buttons function differently in different programs, as well. To program these, go to* **Start > Settings > Control Panel > Wacom Tablet > Tablet Buttons**.

You will notice buttons for **pen mode** *and* **mouse mode**. *The pen mode makes the cursor jump to the location on the screen which corresponds to the location on your tablet. In mouse mode, you have to drag the pen to make your cursor move.*

I cannot imagine any circumstance in which I would want to use mouse mode. I did try it, hated it, and then was unable to change it back on the tablet. I had to go to **Control Panel > Wacom Tablet > Tablet Buttons** *in order to change it back.*

Using the tablet to shade an object

Think of a common or garden ellipse - we are going to add dimension to it using the tablet.

1. To create the illusion of depth, we will need to add two things: shadow and highlight, so start by creating two layers and name them such.

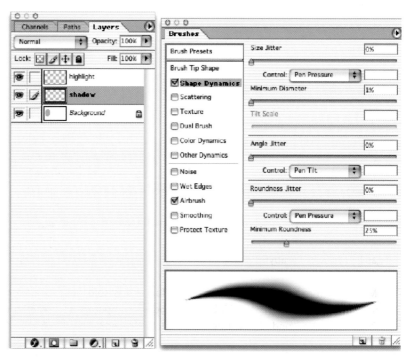

2. Choose the shadow layer. Pick the Brush tool, and check the **Airbrush** option at the top toolbar. Choose black as your color and a large brush, say 300 px.

3. With the area selected to protect the outside area, begin to paint in the shadow. Start soft and slowly build up the shadows using repeated strokes.

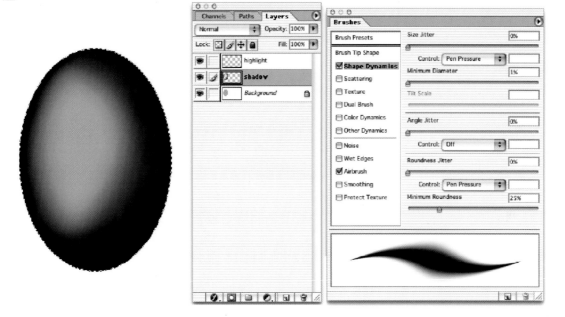

4. Now choose the highlight layer and select white as your color. Paint in the highlights in the same way.

5. To finish it off, add a bright white dot to simulate a reflected highlight.

Notice here the two most important settings for the tablet pen are **Opacity** and **Flow**:

- The opacity jitter will make your paint more opaque the harder you press.

- The flow jitter controls how much ink comes out and how fast. The result is harder or softer edges.

Here is our final picture after just a couple of minutes with the graphics tablet. I know this is a simple example. Imagine the possibilities!

8

The Pen's Eraser: *In Photoshop, the Eraser works just as if you had chosen the Eraser tool from the toolbar. It uses whatever brush tip you last used for your Eraser. In Word and Outlook, to name two, you can use the Eraser to delete text. Just highlight it and it is gone.*

Far more frequently than I would care to admit, I have struggled to accomplish a task with my pen upside down, attempting to attack the problem with the eraser end. There are some functions that will not work with the eraser end. So if your pen "stops working" that is one thing to check first.

Processor

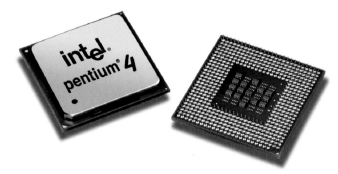

The processor is the actual brain of the computer. This is a small microchip surrounded by huge fans and other cooling devices. In PCs they mostly come in two basic flavors: Intel and AMD.

What speed processor do I need to run Photoshop?

Unfortunately this is another one of those "the faster, bigger and more expensive, the better" situations. PCs and Macs tend to use the processor in very different ways, which means processor speeds (measured in Megahertz or MHz for short) are not really comparable.

For a PC, Photoshop will run fine on anything above 800MHz; anything slower will mean a fair amount of waiting while rendering filter effects. If you're running Photoshop on an old PC, try to make sure that the processor has MMX capability. This means it has built-in dedicated pipelines for multimedia processing which Photoshop will use to its advantage.

On a Mac, anything above 500MHz should do well, ideally in a G4 or at least a G3. You can manage to run Photoshop on both PCs and Macs with slower processors if you increase the RAM.

8

Peripherals

How can I import images into Photoshop?

Scanners and **Digital Cameras** are common tools to use in conjunction with Photoshop. It is important to ensure that these devices and any accompanying software are correctly connected, installed and working properly. The first thing to do when importing images is to install all the correct drivers. Photoshop makes use of the **TWAIN** interface, (it is alleged that TWAIN stands for Technology Without An Interesting Name, but I'm never sure whether to believe it). Basically, TWAIN is an interface between your hardware and software that works across any platform which is used for acquiring images captured by certain scanners, digital cameras, and frame grabbers.

Most Macintosh devices come with plug-ins that make the device accessible without using TWAIN – the plug-in will show up under the **File > Import** menu as an option.

The TWAIN should come with a Source Manager and a TWAIN data source, which will enable it to work with Photoshop and ImageReady.

When you click on **File > Import**, Photoshop will fire up the appropriate software and then import the image into Photoshop. If you're using Windows ME or XP, Photoshop has a crack at importing the image directly using **WIA** (**Windows Image Acquisition**) support.

This is set up in the following way:

- Install the drivers which come with your digital camera or scanner.

- Go to **File > Import** and either select the TWAIN source (you might have more than one such device installed) or just select the correct device from the WIA menu (if you're using Windows ME or XP).

Before you start importing, it's a good idea to think about what you're trying to achieve. Think about the resolution – is the image destined for web or print? Although you *can* increase the image size while in Photoshop, you risk losing quality. By scanning it in at the right resolution in the first place you will get *far* better results.

Customizing your workspace

What is dual monitor support?

Dual monitor support is where you use two monitors instead of one. Large monitors such as 21-inch ones are still fairly pricey and outside the budget of many designers. When you upgrade your monitor, why not keep the old one and connect them both up to your computer? Or you

8

could buy two smaller monitors straight off. In terms of square inches the screen area of one 21-inch monitor is still greater than that of two 14-inch monitors, but you will find that the two monitors will give you more flexibility in arranging your windows.

All that's required is an extra display adapter (or a display adapter that supports using two monitors) and a spare monitor. Upgrading to another 14-inch monitor is a lot cheaper than going out and buying a 21-inch one! If you are using a new card, you should not have problems using dual monitors, but some old cards won't work this way.

If you are working with one monitor that is not as good as the other, you can configure this to good advantage. Use the good monitor on the left, with Photoshop running there. The second, inferior monitor and display adapter can hold all your palettes on the right hand side.

Setting up dual monitor support

Windows

- First shut down, of course. Then plug the extra display adapter into your computer.

- Plug the extra monitor into this adapter.

- Turn the computer on. Some old cards don't support dual monitors, but if you're buying one these days you shouldn't have any problems.

- Right-click on the Desktop, select **Properties > Settings**.

- You should see a picture of two monitors. Click on the right one (which is probably slightly grayed out) and then use the check box underneath which says **Extend my Windows desktop onto this monitor**. Then you're pretty much done.

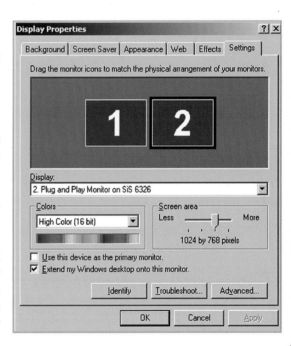

Mac OS

When you hook up a second monitor on the Macintosh, the Monitors Control Panel "senses" the presence of the second monitor. Then you simply position the icons of the two monitors and you're done. Note: it is possible that, by default, the Monitors Control Panel will be set to mirror displays, meaning you'll get the same image on both monitors. Although this is great for presentations with laptops, you'll need to turn this off if you are using the dual monitor set up to extend your workspace,

8

Now open up Photoshop and drag all your palettes onto the right-hand monitor. As you will see, as you move your mouse off the right of the left-hand monitor, it appears on the left side of the right-hand one. An advantage of having two monitors is that you can run them at different resolutions, for example one at 1024x768, and the other at 800x600. This means that you can view your designs in both of the most common monitor resolutions.

Once you have dragged all your palettes to where you're happy with them, use **Window > Workspace > Save Workspace**. Now every time you open up Photoshop it will place your palettes on the right-hand monitor for you.

> *A nice workspace configuration is to have your Layers and History palettes stretched down the screen so that you can see as many layers/history states as possible.*

Although Photoshop *will* open up using the same palette locations each time, saving your workspace is a good idea for these reasons:

- If you change resolution while having Photoshop open it will reset the location of the palettes to their default.

- Instead of then having to drag all your palettes back to where you carefully positioned them, all you need to do is select the name of your workspace that you saved using **Window > Workspace** and choosing the name you gave your workspace.

Everyone knows that a bad craftsman blames his tools, but it really is true that if your equipment and hardware are not up to scratch you'll find Photoshop a lot more frustrating. It's difficult to keep a creative idea alive through numerous crashes, or to get the bigger picture when you're using a tiny monitor. Photoshop is notoriously demanding in terms of power and memory, so you need to be prepared to invest a little to reap huge rewards.

8

Index

The index is arranged hierarchically, in alphabetical order, with symbols preceding the letter A. Many second-level entries also occur as first-level entries. This is to ensure that users will find the information they require however they choose to search for it.

There is an index of tips located after the main index.

3D effects 149

A

Actions palette
modes 225
shortcuts assigned to actions 222
testing actions 224
Add Anchor point tool 44
Adjustment layers 90
evening out fading 121
Hue/Saturation 104
Levels 102
masking 105
retouching photographs 101
selections 65
Adobe Gamma tool 235
Align tools 26
Alpha Channels 63
3D effects 149
saving selections as 50
anchor points
adding and deleting 44
converting straight/curved 44
editing with Direct Selection tool 45
animated GIFs 166

B

Background Eraser 61
background zoom effect 155
Batch Rename option, File Browser 8
blending modes 80, 85
Burn blending modes 81
Dodge blending modes 82
Lighting blending modes 83
blur painting 110
borders
Extract command 57
Quick Mask mode 53
Brush tool
custom brushes 11
shortcuts 12
burn effects
charred layer 158
fire effects 158
removing edges 157
Burn tool
buttons 26

C

cache levels 218
Channel Splitting 118
channels 51
Channels palette
Alpha Channels 50, 63
Levels command 63
selection 62
circles
centering on page 22
concentric circles 23
Cleanup tool 56
clipping groups
avoiding rasterizing type 80
effects 79
Clone Stamp tool
Use All Layers clone option 112
Working Layer clone option 111, 113
color
custom color palettes 204
ICC profiles 234
Pantone Color Matching System 204
previewing text color 14
Swatches palette 204
Color Burn blending mode 81
color casts 128
color correction
color casts 103
Info palette 103
localized correction 104
Color Range option 46
Color Settings dialog box 221
Column Size option 214
composite layers 18
composites
flattened versions for smaller file size 16
saving files as composites 17
Contract option 68
Convert Point tool 44
copyright signature brush 140
Crop tool 99
Hide and Shield option 29
resizing images 30
zooming without losing boundaries 98, 99
Curves 100
Custom Shape tool 202, 203

H

hammered silver effect 151
Hard Light blending mode 83
hardware
  display adapters 232
  graphics tablets 238
  monitors 231, 233
  mouse 237
  peripherals 245
  processors 244
  RAM 227
Healing Brush tool 108
High Pass filter 123
highlights 243
History Brush 59
History States option 209
Horizontal Alignment tool 74
hot silver effect 152
Hue blending mode 84
Hue/Saturation Adjustment Layers 118

I

ICC (International Color Consortium) profiles 234
Image Map tool 193
Image Previews option 210
ImageReady 165
  Animation palette 166
  duplicating frames 166
  Optimize palette 186
  previewing in web browsers 170
  saving animation 170
  slicing images 185, 186, 187
  tweening 167
images
  cropping 29
  flattened versions for smaller file size 16
  navigating 19
  opening multiple 6
  previewing 12
  renaming 7
  renaming batches 8
  rotating 7
importing images into Photoshop 245
Info palette 103
  color correction 103
  Eyedropper 103
Interpolation option 208

L

Lab Color mode 124
Lasso tools 42
Layer controls 77
  Lock all 78
  Lock image pixels 78
  Lock position 78
  Lock transparent pixels 78
layer sets 94, 95
Layer Styles 77
  glassy images 156
  saving 147
  scaling 152, 153, 154
layers
  Adjustment Layers 90
  blending modes 80
  centering 73
  clipping groups 79
  composite layers 18
  creating 71
  creating new documents 76
  Defringe command alternatives 68
  deleting hidden layers 77
  desaturating 81
  duplicating for text shadow effects 72
  filters 78
  finding center of objects 67
  grouping 79
  Layer controls 77
  loading as selections 75
  locking transparency 78
  masks 86
  merging 82, 91, 93
  naming 77
  rasterizing 72
  selections 67
  sets 94
Levels
  adjusting 100
  selections 102
Light blending mode 84
Line tool 73
Linear Burn blending mode 81
Linear Light blending mode 83

M

Magic Wand tool 42, 43

Tips